From the Dust of the Earth - the Earth - Who, Me?

A Study for Reflection

Written & Compiled

Michelle Chopin

ISBN 978-0-692-05223-5

Published in the U.S.A.

Biblical Translations for Comparative Study

With the Word given by the Holy Spirit, the Bible was written over 3500 years ago, between 1445 BC and AD 94 - 96. Through the years verses were remembered, shared, passed down, and transcribed from about forty writers. Multiple translations have been developed for reading and study. The full Bible, from Hebrew, Aramaic, and Greek, has been translated into 636 languages. The Bible is composed of 66 major books and with the apocrypha / deuterocanonical and pseudepigrapha books, includes a total of 84 books.

Millions of people around the globe are still without any translation of the Bible. Thanks to all who continue to translate the Bible.

ASB/NASB/NAS
New American Standard Bible
Scripture taken from the NEW AMERICAN STANDARD BIBLE®,
Copyright© 1960, 1962, 1963, 1968, 1971, 1972, 1973, 1975, 1977, 1995
by The Lockman Foundation.
Used by permission.

BBE/BEB
Basic Bible in English
In the Public Domain.

RHE
Douay-Rheims Bible
In the Public Domain.

ESV
English Standard Version
Scripture quotations are from The Holy Bible, English Standard Version® (ESV®),
copyright © 2001 by Crossway, a publishing ministry of Good News Publishers.
Used by permission. All rights reserved.

GNB
Good News Bible
Scriptures and additional materials quoted are from the Good News Bible ©
1994 published by the Bible Societies/HarperCollins Publishers Ltd UK, Good
News Bible© American Bible Society 1966, 1971, 1976, 1992.
Used with permission.

Table of Contents

"Let all things be done decently and in order."

I Corinthians 14:40   WEB

Theme: Introduction

Opening

"The vision still has its time,

presses on to fulfillment

and it will not disappoint

and if it delays,

wait for it."

"It will surely come.

It will not be late."

Habbakuk, in Babylon
612 BC
Son of Joshua
Tribe of Levi
Musician in Solomon's Temple
Habbakuk 2:3 NAB

Notes

_____

_____

_____

_____

_____

_____

_____

Theme: Archeology

The Chi Rho Symbol

The Chi Rho symbol has "A" and "Ω".
They are the first and last letters
of the Greek alphabet, alpha and omega
(similar to "A" and "Z" in English alphabet).

This symbol appears in the dust
of the Roman Catacombs.

"I am the Alpha and the Omega..."
Rev. 1:18   NIV

"...I am the beginning and the end..."
Rev. 21:6   NIV

"...I am the first and the last..."
Rev. 22:13   NIV

"...who is, and who was, and who is to come..."
Rev. 1:8   NIV

"I am the Alpha and the Omega,
who is,
and who was
and who is to come,
the Almighty."
Rev. 1:8   NIV
John, Apostle
6 AD – 100 AD
from prison, age 90,
on the island of Patmos

"I am who I am."
Exodus 3:14   ESV

Theme: Beginning

Foreword

As a child, I remember learning how to communicate and to clearly express my feelings as an act of trial and error. In the chant, "sticks and stones may break my bones but words will never hurt me," came a realization of the power words had. In truth the lyrics proclaimed harm was being felt by the victim and in actuality the persuasiveness of the rhyme often did little to deter the assailant; but ultimately words do make a difference. The lesson gained from this revelation became reality...communicating and the use of words to express a feeling or a message, and to utilize knowledge are paramount for living life to its fullest.

How do you say "no" to someone whose communication embodies effervescence for life with the desire to help others?

When my friend and colleague, Michelle Chopin, asked me to proofread her manuscript, a work of faith, diligent thought, and inspirational wisdom, I felt not only honored and privileged but compelled to do so. Michelle, a woman of God, whose experiences and lessons of life have offered direction, advice, and solace for many, can now be offered to others through a contemplative format of this book. She has crafted thoughts, feelings, and knowledge, in multiple forms of writings, with an inspiring use of words, hers and those of others. Michelle imparts learning about life, life's meaning, and the possibilities of potential change for one's self; to live life to the fullest.

I invite you to enjoy these writings and allow these words to deliver a unique meaning to life intended just for you.

Sr. Ann Middlebrooks, SEC

Notes

_____

_____

_____

_____

_____

_____

_____

Theme: Purpose

Objectives

Reflection.

Deliberate thought and contemplation
toward opening the window of self-awareness.

Expressions of hopes, dreams, realities
and visions for the future.

Words for those who need help,
for those who are searching and
for those who want confirmation.

Notes

Theme: Credibility

Context

Comprehensive credibility delivers a sustainable impact and strengthens belief. Excerpts, quotes, and bible verses were specially selected and compiled. Verses were compared and studied across multiple biblical translations.

The author has developed creative and educational writings:
>   -to grasp the readers' attention
>   -to spark interest and provoke thought
>   -to encourage reading and promote study
>   -for counseling, guidance, and motivation
>   -for leadership, management and service.

Permissions

The author has made every effort to secure permissions to reprint items contained herein.

We are grateful for those thinkers and writers throughout time who through the wonder of reason and rhyme, inspire us, touch our heart, awaken our imagination, spark the questions we keep inside, speak to us gently, or deeply stir our whole being and then, move each of us forward.

Notes

_____

_____

_____

_____

_____

_____

_____

Theme: Inspiration

Acknowledgements

I am truly grateful to those whose spoken and written word formed lasting impressions in my mind and inspired me to begin this work. I heard you, listened well and made mental notes. Those who believe in and see miracles and share their stories have been a blessing to me.

It is my thought that miracles confuse science. Yet, it is then when things are made crystal clear.

Special thanks to those mentioned below, whom through their experiences and words moved me to write. This writing process has renewed my mind, body and spirit. Master Leaders and Life is Good were each a great inspiration. It was upon reading Blink that I began to write. Sincere thanks to:

Fr. Richard Lombard	George Barna with Bill Dallas
Julia Doolin	Richard Glaubman and George Dawson
Lawrence Wiltz	Malcolm Gladwell

I greatly appreciate my daughter, Camille Chopin, for reading my work and making recommendations, as well as for proofreading and editing. In addition, thanks to Jennifer Hall for her typing.

I am thankful for my husband's love, patience, and understanding, and for his assistance in final proofreading and editing of this work.

Many thanks to Jane Snyder for the time she spent with me to look at and discuss my work, from which I gained valuable ideas. I also thank her for encouraging me to press on toward publication.

I am sincerely grateful for the interest that Sr. Ann Middlebrooks gave to reviewing my manuscript, to write the foreword, and for her kind words. Her suggestions with bibliographic detail were quite helpful.

To Paul Navarre, for sharing with me about writing his book and for making that long distance phone call to refer me to a publisher, a sincere thank you!

For Ka'Lani O'Shea's perseverance in her typing, I am truly thankful! Ka'Lani was always delightful, steadfast, patient, and was to me a shining light! I wish for her all of the sweetest things in life and pray for God's richest blessings!

I am most grateful to Bishop Michael Duca for reviewing my manuscript, sharing this thoughts, and providing guidance.

"Patience and perseverance have a magical effect
before which difficulties disappear
and obstacles vanish."
John Quincy Adams, U.S. President
1767-1848

"A gentle word, a kind look, a good-natured smile
can work wonders
and accomplish miracles."
William Hazlitt, Writer
1778-1830

"The dream was always running ahead of me.
To catch up, to live for a moment in unison with it,
that is the miracle."
Anais Nin, Author
1903-1977

"The miracle is this – the more we share, the more we have."
Leonard Nimoy, Actor
1931-Present

"The Lord himself will give you a miraculous sign...Immanuel"
Isaiah 7:14   NRSV

Notes

_____

_____

_____

_____

_____

_____

_____

Dedication

This manuscript was written while keeping in mind all of those I love and cherish and to whom I would like to devote more time, attention, love, affection, appreciation and praise, as well as, for many family members and friends whom I think of often, miss and cherish. I wish I could have longer visits and conversations with all of them.

I give thanks to my husband, Ed, for his love, patience, and support; my children, Camille, Kathryn, Paul, and Adam, for their determination and endless reserve of unconditional love; my grandchildren, along with God's richest blessings; my parents, Hyland Packard, for his vigilant prayer and love of science; my mother, Sophie Packard, for her unwavering spirit, tenacity and dedication to education; and for their kindness and generosity of service to so many; and for instilling in us the values of hard work and encouraging us to "make an A"; and my brother, Michael Packard, for his quiet, thoughtful, compassionate reserve and never ending patience.

I often think of my teachers, whose dedication and passion for teaching was evident every day of my education. I am thankful for their care about learning and for expecting excellence from their students. Some who inspired me are: Camille Stroud (Natchitoches High School), Frances Phelps (East Natchitoches Junior High School), Dr. Raymond Baumgardner (Biology) and Dr. Bob Rogé (Physics, Northwestern State University); and Dr. Gary Milford (Clinical Psychology and Counseling, Louisiana Tech University). I also offer a sincere and heartfelt thank you to Mrs. Ascension Smith (First Principal of Caddo Magnet High School.)

For my many friends and colleagues, I am thankful for their kind and loving spirit, for listening, for the work which we accomplished and all of the time we spent together.

I will always be thankful for those who hired me to do a job: Doris Marzette (Registered Dietician, Northwest Louisiana); Dr. John Brewer (Louisiana Tech University, Director Barksdale Air Force Base Campus); Wilson Hood (Director Dietary Department Wadley Regional Medical Center), Texarkana, Texas); Leo Lackie (Administrator) and Beverly Zeller Donahue, R.D. (Nutrition Programs Manager, Coastal Plains Health District, Mississippi State Department of Health) for their confidence and for allowing me to work.

I will be forever grateful to Richea Corbin for trusting me and for allowing me to work things out and again to her and to my parents for helping me when I needed it most.

You all have helped to define who I am. Unbeknownst to you, you have helped prepare me to write this manuscript. Through this process, I have grown. If it weren't for you, I would not have accomplished this work. I am most grateful. Thank you so much!

"Never tire of loyalty and kindness.
Hold these virtues tightly.
Write them deep within your heart."
Proverbs 3:3   TLB

"...we who teach will be judged more strictly."
James 3:1 ESV and KJV

"Upon the subject of education,
not pressuring to dictate any plan or system respecting it,
I can only say that I view it as the most important subject
which we as a people can be engaged in."
Abraham Lincoln, U.S. President
1809-1865

"The prayer of a righteous man is powerful and effective."
James 5:10   NIV

"Our creator is the same and never changes
despite the names given Him by people here and
in all parts of the world.
Even if we gave Him no name at all, He would still be there,
within us,
waiting to give us good on this Earth."
George Washington Carver, Scientist
1864-1943

Notes

About the Author
Who Am I?
What Is On My Mind?
What Path Am I On?

I remember that as a very young child my father and I would have fun imagining and making conversation. He would say to me, "You are a Dodo Bird!" and I'd reply, "No, you are a Dodo bird!" Then we'd repeat those lines to each other again and again - it was great fun! Of course, the Dodo Bird is extinct. I am alive and well! I am okay with myself and I know I am on the right path.

As a child, if I did not speak or respond when spoken to, it was not because I was rude, but that my strength was in strict attention, in listening and in observation. I am still reserved and do not talk much, but a lot is always on my mind. Silence is thinking without saying anything. Moments of silence are quite valuable for rest and contemplation. I do anticipate challenges, enjoy working with something new and different and do prefer having something to do. The feeling of being in a rut gradually causes me to be discontent. Generally, I stay quite busy.

I dearly love working in our yard, planning, planting, pruning, meandering or just sitting outside with a good cup of coffee. Downtime for rest and relaxation benefits health and wellness. Besides my husband, myself and four children in our family are four members of the Genus, "*Felis Domesticus.*" Our four furry felines bring great relaxation, loyal companionship and hilarious comedy.

I will move on, far and beyond my early childhood and even past my high school research paper, on Freud's Psychoanalytic Theory of Behavior, to this manuscript which, in part, is far from being parsimonious or classified as an "Abstract." The expressions travel through the continuum of my belief system to the present moment in time, here and now. The formation of my thoughts comes from stories within my memory, my favorite things, collections, files, notes, quotes, imaginings, impressions and inspirations compiled with ideas and analogies. I am aware that one of my abilities is to pay full attention to someone or something and to hold onto a strong impression such that my mind forms and stores the memories very efficiently.

It is my nature to be patient and to tolerate much, to an extent. However, even now, older, sometimes I close my eyes, take a deep breath and hold on for more patience. As I realize that not everyone has the same interests or motivations, I pray to have the patience that I need. Often, I practice "self-talk" or self-evaluation. Occasionally, I must remember the benefit of silence and the importance of being reserved. I tend to be independent and am competitive with myself. I do not feel the need to compete with anyone else, except the calendar, clock, deadlines and due dates. I don't always follow the crowd. If I am not interested in something or don't want to do something then I may decide not to do it. Generally, I do not move in the same direction of fads or trends and it is easy for me to say, "No." I may be somewhat of a rebel.

Quite honestly, I do admit my impatience with behaviors such as: negativity, flippant attitudes, irresponsibility, and disregard of performance standards, inadequate follow-through and also unnecessary drama. There is no good excuse. Individuals, who exhibit such behaviors, do need help and some recognize and will accept help. Some want help, yet others do not. Some do not want to change.

In <u>Master Leaders</u>, George Barna said that you hire a person for what they know, but fire a person for whom they are. He also gave some excellent advice: "You get what you tolerate." It is difficult when they won't do their work, nor can you make them, yet neither can you fire them.

I recall from a counseling course, that when dealing with others it is imperative to be conscious of two major concepts, the first - to not take away all of a person's defenses, and secondly - to never treat someone like a non-person. Also, a statement I once saw on a bulletin board has stayed with me: "It is easier to leave angry words unspoken, than to mend a heart those words have broken."

I do believe that congruence is important to the functionality of a person, that what the person thinks, feels, says and does fit together. In 1943, theorist Abraham Maslow defined the "Hierarchy of Needs," in his theory of human motivation, in which at the highest point an individual may achieve self-actualization. The concepts of self-actualization (self-fulfillment), congruence and wisdom seem to me very similar - to achieve that higher purpose in life.

About honesty, I wholeheartedly agree with the line by William Shakespeare, "To thine own self be true, and it must follow, as the night the day, thou canst not then be false to any man." The Greek writer, Psaunias, spoke about the power of truth in the ancient but ever remembered proverb "Know thyself," which has an unfathomably deep meaning. Self-analysis or self-evaluation is an effective technique to practice.

I work best and perform a task best when I am mentally organized. Strategies which are essential to me and have consistently made a difference, when working on an assignment, project, program or a conference, are to:
- plan/prepare ahead

- be within my belief system
- arrange, set aside time and place
- identify what is appropriate
- remove clutter
- be open-minded and flexible
- consider and handle challenges
- be firm, decided, definite
- be ready, feel ready
- reduce stress

If the task makes sense to me, I will most likely decide to begin the thing with purpose and to plan to do it well, to finish it. To complete the job, whether small or large, is very important to me. From my studies, of methods of teaching, "Scope and Sequence" run deep in my veins. Always focus on details, logistics and tasks, however, never forget about <u>the people</u>.

Throughout this writing process, I was excited. My adrenaline was pumping! I felt compelled to write and although writing was not difficult, I was not able to write fast enough. I did not feel just a quiet voice inside, but felt a definite urge to DO IT NOW! My mind would multi-task various sections simultaneously.

One of my goals for this manuscript is to create or develop an antecedent for change. Learning is realized by an evident change in behavior, concurrently with a change in thinking - which I hope for, according to your need. To those searching for something, I hope these readings promote contemplation and provide encouragement and guidance. These words come through much thought, reflection and thanksgiving, yet through little deliberation.

Although we each think differently, there are things on which we can be on one accord. My mission here is to help others, while hoping that each person will also help many others, possibly toward an exponential effect. I am writing this to you with Godspeed, now, while I am here and you have time.

"I am part of everything I have read."
Theodore Roosevelt, U.S. President
1858-1919

"Attention is the mother of memory."
Fortune Cookie

"Being entirely honest with oneself is a good exercise."
Sigmund Freud, Neurologist
1856-1939

"Liberty according to my metaphysics is a self-determining power
in an intellectual agent.
It implies thought and choice and power."
John Quincy Adams, U.S. President
1767-1848

"Not that I have already obtained all this, or have been made
perfect...but one thing I do;
Forgetting what is behind and straining toward what is ahead,
I press on toward the goal to win the prize for which God has called
me heavenward in Christ Jesus."
Philippians 3:12-14 NIV

Notes

Preface

Far, far away and a long time ago, I only thought of writing a book and had the idea to name it <u>Hopes, Dreams and Realities</u>. Since then, much time, many experiences and many people have crossed my path. I am older now and am writing, however the content contained within has been refined, hopefully like a fine wine. This is a culmination of memories, simultaneous events, and prevailing factors and themes which have been rumbling in my mind.

After the 2013 New Year's Holiday, I had been sick for about one month and still had not felt well at all. According to my physician, my body had "shut down." Bouts of Benign Paroxysmal Positional Vertigo (BPPV) had disrupted my life. Spatial problems had interrupted me on occasion. My family knows of my struggles. My colleagues may know so too. Thus, a time for discernment had presented itself. Realities aligned in front of me and had my full attention. I viewed them as profound. After some time, I began to feel better. A dawning had occurred, an "ah-ha" moment; reference points lit up, an awakening for me. Not only did I feel much better, but also very energized! I then knew that I must move quickly, that I needed to begin composition and that I must do it in this speck of time.

Thoughts were streaming, flying, of course not at light speed, but almost. With so much going on inside of me, a real sense of urgency absolutely had developed. I realized I had so much to say, so much to share. Not only thoughts, but also words, phrases, sentences, examples, analogies and themes were coming to mind so fast that at times I actually felt dizzy. I felt excited and enthusiastic to have a writing project. My mind was gathering a great deal of information and regrouping many years of experiences. There were lasting impressions still in mind. Things were coming together, making sense to me and my adrenaline was pumping.

Factors had simultaneously come together: from my childhood; thirty-six years of marriage and parenting; my first grandbabies and their most important first visits with me; colleagues just retired and others seriously contemplating it; seniors with multiple needs for loving care, time, conversation, attention, encouragement and friendship; immediate and extended family who have moved further away; concerns for the well-being of my children – for their present and their future; and from the last three books which I'd read.

Of major importance, I discovered prevailing themes within the last three books I read. The information expressed therein was significant to me, valuable at that moment in time: Master Leaders by George Barna with Bill Dallas, Life is So Good by Richard Glaubman and George Dawson, and Blink by Malcolm Gladwell. Yet other important clues, even ever so small, continued to surface only to reinforce the want and the need to write day by day.

These clues, early on, seemed to confirm that I should continue my journey to develop this manuscript. Writing was easy and for this I felt so thankful. One day, a fortune from a fortune cookie reinforced a theme I was working on. Then unexpectedly, I found an old address that I had been thinking about and intended to look for, surprisingly by putting my hand right on it in the very drawer it was in.

An unexpected visit with a retired principal was a most valuable and quite memorable experience. I recognized her, introduced myself and then thanked her for all she had done and for the difference she had made for the students at her school throughout the years. She looked down briefly and gave a very sincere reply, "I hope I made a difference," then looked back up at me and repeated with tears in her eyes, "I hope I made a difference!"

Once I had begun the writing process, I felt relieved to have begun. However, there was no doubt in my mind that I could not rest until I finished. I wanted to be mentally organized. I made notes anywhere and everywhere to keep up with ideas that came. Composition was only possible in bits and pieces of time. Sharpened pencils and blank paper were an antecedent to writing and were kept within reach at all times. My mind would not rest; it continued to think, to work, even into the night; I was constantly writing.

I was compelled to record not only thoughts, but beliefs and feelings as well. When ideas flowed, I needed to record them before possibly losing them. Thank goodness for sticky notes and my old file drawer, a shoebox, holding my favorite things (notes, quotes, verses) which I had saved for years.

With this work, I hope to bring help to many who may be seeking encouragement, guidance or motivation. I am thankful to write, to share my reference points and thoughts and to know that upon completion I will feel contentment and peace. I want to finish this and get the word out soon. Once completed, this will enable me to expand my territory, in hope to reach the many that I think of and want to help. My peers may recognize some of my works. Through the years, some have been revised with this effort.

I have exhausted my mental and physical files. This opportunity has allowed me to thoughtfully and honestly let go and share with you some things which have weighed heavily on my mind. I am tremendously excited and very grateful to offer it to you! As Gladwell wrote in Blink, "It is not simply to explore the hidden reasons of our unconscious. Once we know about how the mind works – and about the strengths and weaknesses of human judgement – it is our responsibility to act."[1]

Are you ready?

Let's settle some dust!

[1]Malcolm Gladwell
Blink, pg. 276
Little, Brown and Company
Hachette Books Publisher

"Oh, that you would bless me indeed, and enlarge my territory,
that your hand would be with me,
that you would keep me from evil,
that I may not cause pain."
I Chronicles 4:10   NKJV

"For the deliberation of mortals are timid,
and unsure are our plans,
and scarce do we guess things on earth,
and what is within our grasp we find with difficulty."
Wisdom 9:13-18   NAB

"In an increasingly fast-moving and volatile world, organizations have got to do better at changing or morphing to the next stage in their development. But the first step is about creating a sufficient sense of urgency. This sense of urgency is becoming more important, because it keeps people hyper-alert to all of the things that are going on out there that are either opportunities or hazards and will require some adjustments and flexibility and changes inside. When they've got that sense, people are just so much more determined to not only look every day at what's going on, but to act on what they see and to do something about it."
George Barna with Bill Dallas
Master Leaders, pg. 91

Meditations for the Heart and Mind

"Like apples of gold in settings of silver
is a word spoken in right circumstances."
Proverbs 25:11   NASB

"A man's reach should exceed his grasp, or what's a heaven for?"
Robert Browning, Poet
1812-1889

"The writer needs to react to his or her own internal universe,
to his or her own point of view,
if he or she doesn't have a personal point of view,
it's impossible to be a creator."
Manuel Puig, Author
1932-1990

"Creativity is the greatest expression of liberty."
Bryant H. McGill, Author
1969-Present

"Let us dare to read, think, speak and write."
John Quincy Adams, U.S. President
1767-1848

Theme: Excellence

Aim Higher!

What expectations do you have for yourself?
What are they?
Do you have any?
What are your goals?
What were your New Year's Eve resolutions?

What are you doing?
Where are you going?
What is your mission?
Think on these things.
What difference do you want to make?

Talk to yourself.
Make time for yourself.
Take charge. Persevere.
Put in the time. Make it count.
Don't limit yourself.

Use your creativity. Imagine.
Expand your talents and skills.
Work hard! Strive for
all that you can be!
Aim for Excellence!

What are your expectations of others?
Always hold high expectations.
Never less.
Why would you?
Help them to aim higher, too.

"The quality of a person's life
is in direct proportion to their commitment to excellence,
regardless of their chosen field of endeavor."
Vincent T. Lombardi, Coach
1913-1970

"Quality is not an act. It is a habit."
Aristotle, Philosopher
384 BC-322 BC

"Champions aren't made in gyms.
Champions are made from something they have deep inside them –
a desire, a dream, a vision.
They have to have last-minute stamina,
they have to be a little faster,
they have to have the skill and the will.
But the will must be stronger than the skill."
Mohammed Ali, Boxer
1942-2016

"Success seems to be connected with action.
Successful people keep moving.
They make mistakes, but they don't quit."
Conrad Hilton, Hotelier
1887-1979

"Eighty percent of success is showing up."
Groucho Marx, Actor, Comedian
1890-1977

Theme: Humility

Assets

Are you using your gifts?

Are you using your assets?

In our going out,

with the words we have to share,

it is not about us.

It is about Him.

It is not for us to take and hold

that care within,

but to share with others,

for us to go and tell and live.

Energized with such a treasure,

some run or sing or shout,

give strength and reassure.

"We are His creation."[1]

His instruments we are.

[1]Rev. Karl Daigle
Pastor

"Whoever exalts himself will be humbled;
and whoever humbles himself will be exalted."
Matthew 23:12   NIV

"And whatever you do; in word and deed,
do everything in the name of the Lord Jesus,
giving thanks to God the Father through Him."
Colossians 3:17   NIV

"But those who hope in the Lord will renew their strength.
They will soar on wings like eagles;
they will run and not grow weary,
they will walk and not be faint."
Isaiah 40:31   NIV

"Knowing is not enough; we must apply.
Willing is not enough; we must do."
Johann Wolfgang Von Goethe, Poet and Statesman
1749-1832

Theme: Nurture Yourself

"It's A Blue Day!"[1]

Schedule it! Give yourself a break!
Let your mind and body rest,
free from routine and technology.
Put aside distractions. Relax.
Be patient with yourself.
Create a change – plan ahead – be proactive.
Do something different.
It is good for the body and good for the brain!

Get outside. Look up! Look around!
See the miracles of nature,
falling leaves, colors all around.
Smell the fragrance of flowers in bloom.
Pick some green clover or a delicate dandelion
and blow the seeds up into the air.
See the rising sun, the clear blue sky
and the shapes of the clouds floating by.

Not only, dig in the dirt
but get your hands into the dirt.
Plant some flowers or a garden.
Hear the birds singing,
the crickets chirping.
Feel the warmth of the sun.

Enjoy the small things!
Savor the aroma and flavor of
a cup of fresh hot coffee.
Taste that delicious homemade pie.
Enjoy a glass of freshly brewed iced tea.

Notice your drive
through all green lights.
Listen to the sound of soothing music.
Hold a sweet little baby.
Pet your cat. Play with your dog.
Nibble on a piece of chocolate.
Romance with the full moon.

Recharge yourself.
Take a nap. Awake refreshed.
Exercise. Bend and stretch.
Work on your hobby.
Sip some cool water.

Perk up with an apple, banana or carrot,
some blueberries, honey or yogurt.
Energize with some small red or black beans,
really great whole grain bread and
a little red wine!
Enjoy their anti-aging benefits.

Catch your breath.
Smile and keep moving.
The smile is for you and
the smile is for others, too!

Surround yourself with color.
See color everywhere!
Work toward balance, harmony and variety
for your physical, mental, and spiritual wellness.

Though silence may be difficult to achieve,
being silent may be harder even still.
Seek the sound of silence
for 5-10 minutes each day and
Reward yourself occasionally –
you deserve it!

Nurture yourself.
You are the only one who can take care of <u>you</u>!
This day,
enjoy the sky of blue
and the colors all around you!

[1]"It's a Blue Day!"
Paul Harrington
1985-Present

"Look around you.
There are many things to see, that some would say could never be.
These things I know.
It's true and I will tell you so. They are there to see, if you believe."
Will Huygen, Dutch Author
1922-2009

"A smile is the shortest distance between two people."
Victor Borge, Comedian
1909-2000

"Twenty years from now you will be more disappointed
by the things that you didn't do
than by the ones you did do.
So, throw off the bowlines. Sail away from safe harbors.
Catch the trade winds in your sails.
Explore. Dream. Discover."
Mark Twain, Author
1835-1910

"Whatever is good for your heart is good for your brain,
and whatever is good for your brain is good for your heart."
Daniel G. Amen M.D., Psychiatrist
1954-Present

"A garden to walk in and immensity to dream in –
what more could he ask?
A few flowers at his feet and above him the stars."
Victor Hugo
Les Miserables

Theme: Preparing the Way

Bridges

Are you building bridges?
Reinforce the path.
Share your journey.

The Bridge Builder

"An Old man, going a lone highway,
Came at the evening, cold and gray,
To a chasm, vast and deep and wide,
Through which was flowing a sullen tide.
The old man crossed in the twilight dim.
That sullen stream had no fears for him.
But he turned, when he reached the other side,
And built a bridge to span the tide.
"Old man," said a fellow pilgrim,
"You are wasting strength in building here.
Your journey will end with the ending day;
You never again must pass this way.
You have crossed the chasm, deep and wide,
Why build you the bridge at the eventide?"
The builder lifted his old gray head.
"Good friend, in the path I have come, "he said,
"There followeth after me today
A youth whose feet must pass this way.
This chasm that has been naught to me.
To that fair-haired youth may a pitfall be.
He too, must cross in the twilight dim;
Good friend, I am building the bridge for him."

"Miss Will" Allen Dromgoole, Author and Poet 1860-1934
From the files of Pat Lewis (cousin of "Miss Will") and Ann Chopin
(family friend)

"Constant kindness can accomplish much,
as the sun makes ice melt,
kindness causes misunderstanding, mistrust, and hostility
to evaporate."
Albert Schweitzer, Theologian
1875-1965

"The great thing in this world is not where we stand,
but what direction we are heading."
Oliver Wendell Holmes, Writer
1809-1894

"Teach me to do your will, for you are my God,
may your good Spirit lead me on level ground."
Psalms 143:10 NIV

"Therefore we do not lose heart.
Though outwardly we are wasting away,
yet inwardly we are being renewed day by day."
II Corinthians 4:16 & 18 NIV

". . . how God anointed Jesus of Nazareth
with the holy Spirit
and power.
He went about doing good and healing all those
oppressed by the devil,
for God was with Him."
from Peter's Speech
Acts 10:38 NABRE

Theme: Live

Celebrate Life!

Find moments to celebrate every day!
Be thankful and express gratitude.
Take time. Slow down.
Simplify your life.

Play with your children, your grandchildren,
or your beloved pet.
Give a smile and a hug to your loved ones.
Have coffee, dessert and great conversation!
Encourage others. Dust them with praise.

Calm down. Take a break. Go outside.
Take a brisk walk or a relaxed stroll.
View nature's beauty.
Bike, jog, swim, dance.
Collect photos, cards, quotes, cartoons.

Look for the positive. De-stress.
Talk about and remember the good times you've had!
Plan ahead and find more to celebrate.
Time marches on. So, do it now.
Create wonderful memories.

Celebrate life!
You are unique and specially made.
You are an amazing person!
Be thankful every day.

"O give thanks unto God for He is Good,
His mercy endureth forever."
Psalms 107:1 KJB

"Work is good provided you do not forget to live."
Bantu Proverb

"Think excitement, talk excitement, act out excitement
and you are bound to become an excited person.
Life will take on a new zest, deeper interest, and greater meaning."
Norman Vincent Peale, Author
1898-1993

"Those who bring sunshine to the lives of others
cannot keep it from themselves."
James Barrier, Author
1860-1937

"Finally, brothers, whatever is true, whatever is honorable,
whatever is just, whatever is pure,
whatever is lovely, whatever is commendable,
if there is any excellence, if there is anything worthy of praise,
think about these things."
Philippians 4:8 ESV

"I praise you,
for I am fearfully and wonderfully made.
Wonderful are your works; that I know very well."
Psalms 139:14 NRSV

Theme: Happiness

Choice

Happiness is a choice.
Accept that happiness is your own
God-given responsibility.
Happiness lies within.
You hold the key.

Don't wait for an offer of, 'I'm sorry.'
Just forgive and love anyway
without conditions or contingencies.
Forgive others. Forgive your child.
Forgive your parents.
Forgive yourself.

Take care of yourself. Love yourself.
Be your own best friend. "Rescue yourself."[1]
Develop a balance between faith, family and friends.
Develop friendships - a support system.
You are not alone. Do for others. Volunteer.
Focus. Avoid distractions. Remove clutter (cobwebs).

Identify and select your goals.
Happiness is an ongoing, continuous effort,
a never-ending process, along your continuum.
Nourish your soul!
Be content with what you have.
Show gratitude daily.

Turn the key...be more optimistic.
Realize your personal achievement.
Feel more joy, happiness and satisfaction.
You will enjoy feeling progress toward your goals.

Don't forget.
Be ready!
You always hold the key.
It is inside of you!
Believe in Yourself!

Be a genuinely happy person!

[1]Rev. Karl Daigle,
Pastor

"Happiness depends upon ourselves."
Aristotle, Philosopher
384 BC-322 BC

"Most people are about as happy as they make up their minds
to be."
Abraham Lincoln, U.S. President
1809-1865

"Happiness is not the absence of conflict,
but the ability to cope with it."
Anonymous

"Happiness is an attitude of mind,
born of the simple determination to be happy
under all outward circumstances."
J. Donald Walters, Author and Yoga Guru
1926-2013

"Don't Worry. Be Happy."
Originally by Meher Baba, Indian Mystic
1894-1969
Sung 9/1988 by Bobby McFerrin, Musician

"Happiness lies in the joy of achievement and
the thrill of
creative effort."
Franklin Roosevelt, U.S. President
1882-1945

Notes

Theme: Communication

Conversation

When another person is talking to you,
how long do you listen?
What then, are you thinking about?
Are you still listening?
Do you distract yourself? Don't!

Be mindful of the individual
with whom you are engaged in conversation.
Hang in there! Be attentive.
Make eye contact - it will help tremendously.
Listen to and talk with the person.

Conversation is interactive.
It is a dialogue - not a monologue.
Interaction occurs best when messages are
sent and received through
mutually satisfactory,
two-way, effective communication.

"Be mindful of the Conversational Triplet.
It will help and
it will make a difference!" [1]

"Every conversation has an afterlife of
those individuals and in the experiences of
those affected by it." [2]

Avoid unnecessary assumptions,
unfounded, which may draw
incorrect explanations,
from lack of conversation.

[1] Dr. Mike Hemphill, Speaker
Provost and Dean Centenary College
(7/1/2010 Honor's Reception)

[2] Hilda Carpenter, Ph.D.
Human Development and Communication
Fielding Graduate University, 2006-07

"Be impeccable with your word.
Speak with integrity.
Say only what you mean.
Avoid using the word to speak against yourself or
to gossip about others.
Use the power of your word in the direction of truth and love."
Miguel Angel Ruiz, Author
1952-Present

"Avoid compulsively making things worse."
Fortune Cookie

"Always be kind,
for everyone is fighting a battle."
Plato, Philosopher
427 BC-347 BC

"The wise in heart are called discerning
and gracious words promote instruction."
Proverbs 16:21   NIV

"Proper responses bring salvation to many
and glory to God."
Fr. Thomas Elavunkal, CMI,
Pastor

Notes

Theme: Leadership and Organizational Performance

Cornerstone – The Foundation

What Defines an Organization or Workgroup?
   Goals - the mission
   Values - the importance of policies and procedures, high
            expectations
Integrity - the implementation of the program, exceptional quality and
            accountability, sound policies and practices
   Culture - the established behaviors and methods, how employees do
            what they do best

What Defines the Culture of the Organization?
            - how employees attain their mission with consistent success
            - the totality of behavior patterns, interactions, cognitive
             constructs
            - characteristics common to the particular group
            - the cumulative deposit of knowledge, experience, beliefs,
             values, attitude
            - the product of work and thought

What Supports or Sustains the Organization?
            - a shared vision between leadership and employees
            - a positive environment
            - a productive team

   Leaders
            - create the vision
            - determine the plan and goals
            - are visible, interactive and engaged
            - observe and listen well
            - clearly care about employees
            - build a cohesive group
            - reinforce teamwork
            - provide for and support continued success

- recognize employee success
- make the tough decisions

Communication
- is professional and positive
- is consistent and confident
- tone is clear not curt
- is focused on target
- informs employees of changes

Resolution
- to overcome obstacles
- to resolve conflict
- to be proactive

Employees
- embrace the mission
- are prompt and present
- are dependable
- are efficient, with time on task
- understand goals and expectations
- desire to learn and contribute
- listen and have a valued voice
- succeed and target excellence
- accept increased responsibility
- adapt to change

What Validates Organizational Improvement?
Successful Strategies include
- a network of business relationships
- ongoing quality assurance program
- planned promotional activities and events
- clear and regular outreach
- education, training, teambuilding
- investment in safety
- available health and wellness activities

- responsive support and counseling
- consideration and evaluation of new ideas
- a sense of timing

Successful Strategies
- ensure the continuity of the mission, goals, values and vision, even across transition of staffing, remaining ever strong and even stronger as an organization
- assess team member strengths and delegate to benefit from effective outcome

Marketing and Merchandising can
- offer a gesture of friendship
- add a unique or personal touch
- set the organization apart

What Are the Building Blocks of Careers?
- accuracy, fairness, honesty, timeliness and trust

A 'BIG' Career Success Factor is TIME MANAGEMENT.

With the Cornerstone Set for Successful Leadership
- employees trust and respect the leader, know the leader cares and participate in consistent and effective training all critical to meet employee needs and organizational goals.

The Cornerstone Set With a Firm Foundation
- administrators, leaders and managers have employees who achieve and follow.

"We will not succeed, we will not survive,
if we fail to find unity in our values, our culture,
and our purpose as an organization."
Hugh L. McColl, Jr., CEO
1935-Present

"Outstanding leaders go out of the way
to boost self-esteem of their personnel.
If people believe in themselves, it's amazing what they can accomplish."
Sam Walton, Businessman
1918-1992

"The supreme quality for leadership is unquestionably integrity.
Without it, no real success is possible,
no matter whether it is in a section gang, on a football field,
in an army,
or in an office."
Dwight D. Eisenhower, U.S. President
1898-1969

"It's not a matter of just technical competence, it is imagination.
It's creativity. It's intellect. A problem solving mentality.
We must have the best talent, the most talented people. And that
said, we'd better keep them when we get them, as well as we can,
because we're going to need them."
Mike Cook, CEO

"The best <u>executive</u> is the one who has enough sense to pick good
people to do what he wants done, and self-restraint enough to keep
from meddling with them while they do it."
Theodore Roosevelt, U.S. President
1858-1919

"Favoritism may lead to corruption."
Rev. Richard J. Lombard, Associate Pastor

"To educate a person in mind and not in morals
is to educate a menace to society."
Theodore Roosevelt, U.S. President
1858-1919

Notes

_____

_____

_____

_____

_____

_____

_____

Theme: Set an Example

Counsel

William Hettler, (Director of University Services, University of Wisconsin, Stevens Point) Keynote Speaker at the 1991 American Association for Counseling and Development Convention, told counselors that most human behavior has one of three effects: enhancing, destroying, or making no difference. He said that counselors must be in the first category because they have the capacity to improve society, but that most people fall into the third category. Hettler said we need to teach children coping and survival skills. He reminded counselors to set an example – to practice what they preach and said that <u>we</u> need to look out for each other.
"Our behaviors set the norms for our children. They will carry on our mistakes if we don't change. They are our hope for the future," he said.
"Don't take yourself too seriously, laugh, have fun and be kind to other people," was his <u>Prescription for Wellness</u>. He read this poem to those attending:

> "I'd rather see a sermon
> Than hear one any day.
> I'd rather one would walk with me
> Than merely show the way.
> The eye's a better pupil
> And more willing than the ear;
> Fine counsel is confusing
> But examples' always clear.
> I soon can learn to do it,
> If you'll let me see it done.
> I can see your hands in action,
> But your tongue too fast may run;
> And the lectures you deliver
> May be very fine and true.

But I'd rather get my lesson
By observing what you do.
For I may misunderstand you
And the high advice you give,
But there's no misunderstanding
How you act and how you live." [1]

[1]William Hettler, MD, Speaker
National Wellness Institute
1991 AACD Convention

"The child becomes what he is taught;
hence we must watch what we teach and how we live."
Jane Addams, Author
1860-1935

"Children need models rather than critics."
Joseph Joubert, Writer
1754-1824

"If you raise your children
to feel that they can accomplish any goal or task they decide upon,
you will have succeeded as a parent and
will have given your children
the greatest of all blessings."
Brian Tracy, Author
1944-Present

"What you do has a far greater impact than what you say."
Stephen Covey, Author
1932-2012

"Don't take yourself too seriously, laugh, have fun
and be kind to other people."
William Hettler, MD, Speaker
1943-Present

Notes

Theme: Accomplishment

Difference?

You are here, now.
You ask, "Have I made a difference?
What have I done? What did I accomplish?
Have I made a difference?"

You've had an opportunity
to help someone, to impact someone's life,
to improve their livelihood.
Daily, with your visibility, interest,
with your smile, encouragement, kind word,
with your eye contact, listening ear,
by really seeing and working with that person -
the answer is, Yes!
You have made a difference!

Through your teaching,
 training, time and attention,
you have been there for each one.
You have been there for them.

For any given moment, hour, day,
we are only present.
We are here, now.
Make it count.
What is inside you? Share it!

Press on toward the goal
with the calling you have
throughout the course of each day.
We need inspiration and motivation.
People need you!

"You can accomplish much if you do not care who gets the credit."
Abraham Lincoln, U.S. President
1809-1865

"Treat people as if they were what they ought to be
and you will help them to become what they are capable of being."
Johann Wolfgang Von Goethe, Poet & Statesman
1749-1832

"A leader's <u>courage </u>to fulfill his vision comes from passion
not position."
John Maxwell, Author
1947-Present

"Courage is what preserves our liberty, safety, life and our homes
and parents, our country and children.
Courage comprises all things."
Plautus, Playwright
254 BC-184 BC

". . . proclaim the word;
be persistent whether it is convenient or inconvenient;
convince, reprimand, encourage through all patience
and teaching."
II Timothy 4:2 NABRE

Theme: Extinction

The Dodo Bird
Discovered and Extinct in one Century

The Dodo bird was not a mythical creature. Dodo birds enjoyed life on the paradise island of Mauritius, east of Madagascar in the Indian Ocean. As they enjoyed the easy life and plenty of food, neither hassled by competitors for food nor worried about predators looking to eat them, they became lazy. Thus, the Dodos needed not to adapt for flight but only to scavenge for fruits. They feasted on fruits from fallen trees, bulbs, nuts, palm fruits and seeds. Since they were flightless birds, they nested and rested on the ground, needing no refuge. At 3.3 feet tall, 44 pounds and a quite large and wide beak, the Dodo was a strange looking bird.

Unfortunately, their life of leisure too soon was interrupted. In 1581, the strange gray creature with yellow feet, a naked head, a black, green and yellow beak and a tuft of tail feathers was discovered! In 1598, a Dutch sailor recorded his sightings and observations of the Dodos. So, then it was on! They were such an easy catch. The birds were preyed upon not only by sailors, but also by the sailors' pets who had invaded their domain. The poor Dodos did not survive the hunt. The last sightings of the birds were recorded in 1662 by a Dutch mariner who had shipwrecked and then once again, in 1688 by a hunter.

The fact that an entire species which was discovered, however extinct within only one century was of major significance and drew great attention from such an impact of human intervention. Man had destroyed them all. The defenseless Dodo had disappeared from the Earth.

Thanks to 17th century paintings and written accounts of the Dodo bird, we have a visual idea of the bird's appearance.

A 2005 expedition found sub fossil remains of the bird, along with those of other animals, within evidence of a flashflood. The most complete and best preserved skeleton was discovered in a cave, as recently as June 2007. Frederick William Frohawk found the specimen in a cave in Mauritius. "Fred," the Dodo bird, is maintained and on display in the Natural History of Museum in London.

The Life Line or the lasting ability of a thing is dependent upon not only extraneous variables but, moreover upon an intrinsic nature or innate qualities.

The Sustainability, or the existence of a thing, requires both preservation (maintenance, protection, and conservation) and sustenance (support and strength) of life.

"HAVOC and DEMOLITION are in the Air!"
My line from our high school play,
<u>The Fish Mongers</u>

"What we anticipate seldom occurs;
what we least expect generally happens."
Benjamin Disrael, Prime Minister of Great Britain
1804-1881

"Let us form one body, one heart, and defend to the last warrior
our country, our homes, our liberty and the graves of our fathers."
Tecumseh, Tribal Chief
1768-1813

"The Dodo used to walk around,
And take the sun and air,
The sun yet warms his native ground,
The Dodo is not there!
The voice which used to squawk and squash
Is now forever dumb -
Yet may you see his bones and beak
All in the Mu-se-um."
Hiliare Belloc, Poet
1870-1953
<u>The Bad Child's Book of Beasts</u>

"The severest justice may not always be the best policy."
Abraham Lincoln, U.S. President
1809-1865

Notes

Theme: Planet Earth

Dust
Our Dust and God's Dust

When I was very young, I clearly recall a serious discussion between my mother and my uncle. I have a visual memory of them still, on the back porch of our house. Although I vaguely remember the subject, the tone and length of discussion I do remember well.

Somewhat concerned, I emphatically spoke up to interrupt them and said, "Two pieces of dirt can't fuss!" which immediately ended their philosophical dissertation.

"Every saint and sinner
in the history of our species lived there –
on a mote of <u>dust</u>
suspended on a sunbeam."
Carl Sagan, Astronomer
1934-1996

"And then the Lord God formed man of the dust of the ground,
and breathed into his nostrils the breath of life;
the man became a living soul."
Genesis 2:7   KJB

"The first man was of the dust of the earth
and the second man is of heaven.
1 Corinthians 15:47   NIV

"I am inclined to think that the far greater part, if not at all,
of these difficulties which have hitherto amused philosophers,
and blocked up the way to knowledge,
are entirely owing to ourselves that we first raised a dust and then
complain we cannot see."
George Berkeley, Philosopher
1685-1753
Bishop of Cloyne, Dublin Ireland

"Give me the liberty to know, to utter, and to argue freely
according to conscience, above all liberties."
John Milton, Poet
1608-1674

"The Lord is merciful and loving,
slow to become angry and full of constant love.
He does not keep on rebuking; He is not angry forever.
As high as the sky is above the earth,
so great is His love for those who honor him.
As far as the east is from the west,
so far does he remove our sins from us.
As a father is kind to his children,
so the Lord is kind to those who honor him.
He knows what we are made of; he remembers that we are dust."
Psalms 103:8-9, 11-14. ASB

Notes

_____

_____

_____

_____

_____

_____

_____

Theme: Mission

Every Day

Why am I here?

We are here to serve the children and others,

If your mind and heart are open
you can find a mission
and build upon it every day
with someone, at some place, at some time,
then continue that ongoing rapport,
that work in progress.

When do you have a caring feeling?
You do not have to go far to see
that young person working so diligently,
that older person struggling to get around.
Do you notice them?
When do you have a caring heart?

Remove obstacles. Simplify details.
Spend more time with those who need it.
Listen more. Talk more. Do more.
Move forward. Don't stop.
Carry forth.

People live and move and need, every day.
Be sensitive to the needs of others.
Be open-minded.
When does caring move you to act?
When are your hands transformed into helping hands?

Do for them as you can,
then do even more
to continue your mission
every day.

"No obstacles."
Sue Creighton, Educator
1950-Present

"Life is frittered away by detail. Simplify, simplify, simplify."
Henry David Thoreau, Author
1817-1862

"Give me the ready hand rather than the ready tongue."
Giuseppe Garibaldi, Politician
1807-1882

"We ought always thank God for you
because your faith is growing abundantly
and your love for one another increasing."
II Thessalonians 1:3   NIV

"Live a life worthy of the calling you have received."
Ephesians 4:1   NIV

"What builds support? Faithfulness, caring and prayer."
Rev. Richard Lombard
Associate Pastor

Notes

Theme: Watching

Today did you look around?
Did you see God?

Fishing

"I fished every day, all day long. But I'm not one of those fisherman that changes lures and checks their bait every five minutes. Lots of people fish that way. Not me. I put on some chicken livers or maybe some grubs and cast out from shore. I had a bobber up the line that would just sit out in the water. I carried all my gear in a big white bucket. When I was all set, the lid on the bucket was my seat.

I didn't just wait. No! I would be watching, always watching the water. I would look at the water. Most people look at the water but don't really see much. Not me. Every day, I be out there fishing. I look at the water. It's never the same, I just kept watching. That's when I saw what God does. Sometimes the water is so still, sometimes bubbles come up, sometimes the wind comes and the water's got ripples across the surface.

That's what God does. He moves the wind across the water or leaves it still. He can do all that. That's God doing that and He can do it on any lake that He wants to."

Richard Glaubman and George Dawson
Life is So Good. 2000, Random House, NY. Pg. 223

I wish I could have met Mr. George Dawson from Marshall, Texas who learned to read at age 98.

"The old man who could not read lives alone
in a house that is small and square, ...
The old man got by until 1996,
when a young man knocked on his door
and said he was recruiting people
for the Adult Basic Education classes at the old high school.
'I've been alone for 10 years,' the old man told him.
'I'm tired of fishing. It's time to learn to read.'"
Larry Bingham, Journalist
Seattle Times, February 1, 1998
As reprinted by
Richard Glaubman and George Dawson
Life is So Good. 2013, Random House, NY. Pg. 224

"In my heart will ever lie just the echo of a sigh. Good-bye."
Noel Coward, Author
1899-1973

"Few are those who see with their own eyes
and feel with their own hands."
Albert Einstein, Physicist
1879-1955

"For since the creation of the world,
God's invisible qualities – his eternal power and divine nature –
have been clearly seen, being understood
from what has been made,
so that men are without excuse."
Romans 1:20 NIV

"Come and see the works of the Lord."
Psalms 46:8   NIV

"By faith we understand that the universe was formed
at God's command,
so that what is seen was not made out of what was visible."
Hebrews 11:3   NIV

Notes

Theme: Gratitude

Flight

High,
up in this sea of clouds
far above
the earth below,

in light
of what I see,
the question
occurred to me –

'What is
all that we really have?'

The sky above,
the land below,
all of those whom we love,
family, friends and You.

For all of this
I say thank You.

And thank You
for your gentle hand
to set us
so softly down.

"Summer is the annual permission slip to be lazy.
To do nothing and have it count for something.
To lie in the grass and count the stars.
To sit on a branch and study the clouds."
Regina Brett, Author
1956-Present

"Rest is not idleness, and to lie sometimes
on the grass under trees on a summer's day,
listening to the murmur of the water,
or watching the clouds float across the sky,
is by no means a waste of time."
John Lubbock, Banker
1834-1913

"I'm a dreamer.
I have to dream and reach for the stars,
and if I miss a star then I grab a handful of clouds."
Mike Tyson, Boxer
1966-Present

"Be thou the rainbow in the storms of life.
The evening beam that smiles the clouds away,
and tints tomorrow with prophetic ray."
Lord Byron, Poet
1788-1824

"...From the mountains, to the prairies, to the oceans white with foam,
God bless America, my home sweet home..."
Irving Berlin, Composer
1888-1989

Theme: Stewardship

Gifts

Look around
take a moment,
not in the past, not in the future,
just be <u>here</u> and <u>now</u>, fully present.

We have a common mission, you and I.
The children are:
"the heart and soul of what we do.
Our responsibilities include
teaching, service and outreach."[1]

Consider your gifts,
your strengths,
your abilities,
your talents,
your insight.

A good steward of your gifts?
They are freely given
and are not your own.

The power rests inside of you;
it is within your grasp -
It is your decision
to exercise that power and
to use your gifts to grow and
to help others grow.

Share your gifts
with thankfulness and
with a humble spirit.
Invest in others.
Take a moment...
where are you?

[1]Rev. Richard Lombard
Associate Pastor

"We make a living by what we get.
But we make a life but what we give."
Winston Churchill, Prime Minister of Britain
1874-1965

"As each has received a gift,
use it to serve one another as good stewards of
God's varied grace...
to him belong the glory and dominion forever and ever."
I Peter 4:10-11   ESV

"The God who gave us life gave us liberty at the same time."
Thomas Jefferson, U.S. President
1743-1826

"...And I pray that you being rooted and established in love,
may have power together with all the saints
to grasp how wide and long and high and deep is the love of Christ,
and to know this love that surpasses knowledge;
that you may be filled to the measure of all the fullness of God..."
Ephesians 3:17-19   NIV

"A winner is someone who recognizes his God-given talents,
works his tail off to develop them into skills
and uses these skills to accomplish his goals."
Larry Bird, Professional Basketball Player
1956-Present

Notes

Theme: Know

Here

Have you ever asked -
Why am I here?
Why me?
Can I do this?

Ken Melrose, of the Toro Company, contemplated these very questions when he was given a critical job assignment. He knew he needed help and although doubtful, he felt confident he would be okay because he knew he was not alone.

"So I got a sign, framed it, and put it up in my office. I knew that God would not let me do things beyond my own limitations, that He would be there to help me. I figured that somehow this was what God wanted me to do, even though I wasn't so sure I wanted to do it. So I put up a sign that said, 'God meant for you to be here...now!' It was a very visible sign, framed and all, and I put it on the wall opposite my desk so when I'd come into the office, I'd see that sign, first thing. If I was on the phone and I was looking over at this wall, or if I had some people in my office around the table, I could see it."

Ken Melrose, CEO of Toro Company
As quoted by George Barna with Bill Dallas
Master Leaders, p. 161

As I read Ken's story, tears came to my eyes for I'd had similar thoughts and feelings while working in my office and supervising many schools only blocks from where I was born and had lived my early years on Darien and Frederick Streets. Both my background and my work experiences had prepared me for this work.

Challenges occur daily and so many employees and others need help in one way or another. I could not have planned it. God marked my path. So, I too made a sign for my office that says, 'Remember, God wants me to be here!' I placed the small sign on the bookcase directly in front of my desk, where I can see it every day.

Do you know where God wants you?

"If you're not sure where you're going
you're liable to end up some place else."
Robert F. Mager, Ph.D.
1923-Present

"Know thyself."
Pausanias, Ancient Greek Writer
AD 110-AD 180
A Proverb on the Power of Truth

"In Him, we live and move and have our being."
Acts 17:28 NIV

7:15 a.m. Telephone Call:
D. Marzette: "Do you want to work?" M. Chopin: "Yes."
D. Marzette: "Be here at 10:00 a.m." M. Chopin: "Yes ma'am!"
Doris Marzette, Registered Dietitian
Northwest Louisiana

"Let the favor of the Lord our God be upon us,
and prosper the work of our hands -
O prosper the work of our hands."
Psalms 90:17 NRSV

Notes

_____

_____

_____

_____

_____

_____

_____

Theme: People

In a Hurry?

So many people need help.
So many are seeking attention every day.
Whether for companionship,
encouragement, guidance, or support.
Do you see them?
Or are you in a hurry?

Time and time again, we see
the sweet older lady
at the sandwich shop or
at the bank or grocery store or
even at the book store!

The senior, alone,
who is unable to do some things,
do you speak to them?
What do you say?
Are you in a hurry?

When we arrive for a visit
we hear excitement in their voices,
we see the delight in their eyes,
and the smiles on their faces
for our presence, our hugs and
time for some conversation.
They look forward to talking.
They may do all the talking.

We don't have to travel far -
they are right next door,
down the street, around the corner,

or at your next stop.
They are greeting us at church
or taking out our groceries.
We are on the same path.

Take time to look around. Pay attention.
Are you in a hurry? Slow down.
What will you talk about?
People are all around.
Dust them with praise.

"Let us not become weary in doing good,
for at the proper time we will reap a harvest
if we do not give up."
Galatians 6:9 NIV

"In each of us are places where we have never gone.
Only by pressing the limits do you ever find them."
Dr. Joyce Brothers, Psychologist
1927-2013

"Life is all memory except for the one present moment
that goes by so quick you hardly catch it going."
Tennessee Williams, Writer
1911-1983

"Do you not know? Have you not heard?
The Lord is the everlasting God,
the Creator of the ends of the earth.
He will not grow tired or weary."
Isaiah 40:28 NIV

"But encourage one another daily, as long as it is called Today."
Hebrews 3:13 NIV

Notes

_____

_____

_____

_____

_____

_____

_____

Theme: Analysis

Indifference

Regarding an individual's behavior,
we've sometimes heard people say:
"He won't change!" or, "He can't change!"
"What difference would it make?"
Yes! A change will make a difference, one way or another.
The change may not be seen now, but may be seen later.

Why be negative? Why deny the possibility for change?
Such an absolute expression of belief
may quickly turn,
or end the conversation
and present the speaker as,
knowingly, prepared to issue the last word.

There is cause to analyze this.
Sometimes, we may feel afraid,
disappointed, hurt, exasperated,
upset or even angry with someone,
but, such a determination
to claim a limit to God's power
it not for us to do.

We may have knowledge within that construct,
however, not full knowledge, ever,
to limit or to determine God's power.

Realize that along with seeing and hearing,
thinking, sensing, feeling, and judging also
co-exist within a person.
We are still emotional and intellectual beings.

Though we can help many,
for some, we can only pray.
Some don't want help.
They don't want to change.
Though, always, we must hope.

Being flippant helps no one.
Let go of the negative.
Care enough to hope.
Have hope enough to care.

Inside those who hear and listen,
what is going on?
So much!
Do you stop and watch?
Do you stop and listen?

You watch. You listen.
You'll see.
I believe for you.

"Fear defeats more people than any other one thing in the world."
Ralph Waldo Emerson, Writer
1803-1882

"People do not seem to realize that their opinion of the world
is also a confession of character."
Ralph Waldo Emerson, Writer
1803-1882

"God grant me the serenity to accept the things I cannot change,
the courage to change the things I can,
and the wisdom to know the difference."
Reinhold Niebuhr, Theologian
1892-1971
The Serenity Prayer, published 1951

"Our attempts to control God
and keep God safely within our pre-determined categories
are contradicted by the early Christian preaching about Jesus."
Mark Tranvik, Writer
(Commentary on Acts 10:34-43)

"Produce good fruit as evidence of your repentance...
For I tell you, God can raise up children to Abraham
from these stones."
Matthew 3:8 & 9b NRSV

Notes

Theme: Joy

Laughter

People - bubbly, enjoying life, fun to be around,
possess the gift of laughter - the fountain of youth!

Their laugh is contagious, like a hug.
Their sense of humor and happiness bring joy to you and me,
sunshine to our day,
comfort and relaxation to folks all around!

The gift of laughter is therapy at no charge!
It helps people feel better, lifts spirits, reduces stress,
relieves tension, prevents irritability and burnout.

Laughter has healing power!
It increase alertness, creativity, memory,
adrenaline and blood flow to the brain,
lowers blood pressure, exercises abdominal and heart muscles
and boosts the immune system!

Laughter forms a connection between people.
The little things that make us laugh,
we can share with others too, those funny jokes,
stories, cartoons, photos, games, those hilarious
movies and precious videos of children, babies and pets!

Find humor every day. Laugh. Enjoy life!
Humor is powerful!

"For people who like peace and quiet – a phoneless cord."
Fortune Cookie

"Laughter is good for you.
It changes the chemistry in the brain.
It can erase fear, anxiety and depression."
Glenn Plaskin, Writer
"Why Laughter is Good for You"

"If you are too busy to laugh, you are just too busy!"
Anonymous

"A sense of humor is part of the art of leadership,
of getting along with people,
of getting things done."
Dwight D. Eisenhower, U.S. President
1890-1969

"He will yet fill your mouth with laughter and
your lips with shouts of joy."
Job 8:21 NIV

Theme: Commitment

Love

"Commitment is what transforms a promise into reality.

It is the words that speak boldly of your intentions

and the actions which speak louder than the words.

It is making the time when there is none.

Coming through time after time,

year after year after year.

Commitment is the stuff character is made of.

The power to change the face of things.

It is the daily triumph of integrity over skepticism."

Anonymous

"Love is patient, love is kind.
It does not envy, it does not boast,
it is not proud. It is not rude.
It is not self-seeking, it is not easily angered,
it rejoices in the truth,
it keeps no records of wrongs.
It protects, always hopes, always perseveres."
I Corinthians 13:4-7   NIV

"Not everything that can be counted counts,
and not everything that counts can be counted."
Albert Einstein, Physicist
1879-1955

"Be completely humble and gentle; be patient,
bearing with one another in love."
Ephesians 4:2   NIV

"Three things will last forever – faith, hope, and love –
and the greatest of these is love."
I Corinthians 13:13   NLT

"And this I pray, that your love may abound still more and more
in real knowledge and all discernment."
Philippians 1:9-11   NASB

Manager's Tool Kit

Remember,
there is more to being a manager
than knowing the content and
passing the test!

You must possess:
Application – successfully do what you claim to know
People skills – listen, talk, teach, train, enjoy people and teams
Physical and Mental Endurance – keep going, press on, follow through
Attention Span – memory depends upon attention
Attention to Detail – understand and know what the small things are;
manage details well, accurately, timely, and safely.

You must like people
and like working with people,
otherwise, you may need to go do something else.

You must not only know you are the manager,
but that you are the one doing the managing.
Manage your employees,
don't be difficult, guide them,
don't antagonize them.
Remain positive.

Keep instructions clear and concise.
Identify opportunities for success.
Recognize individual success.
Dust with praise.

Always remember,
everyone doesn't need to know everything,
except when absolutely necessary and appropriate.

Possess confidentiality.
It is vital to hold many things in confidence –
you will gain respect.

Take note,
not everyone is okay.
Be alert. Be vigilant.

Most importantly, be consistent.
Be at work.
Look up. Don't look down.
Smile. Listen more. Talk less.
Hold your shoulders back and head up high.
Stand tall! Be confident!

Look in the mirror a second time!
It is better to be starched than wrinkled.
Remember,
action generates inspiration!

"Watch your relations with others carefully. Be reserved."
Fortune Cookie

"Before you are a leader, success is all about growing yourself.
When you become a leader,
success is all about growing others."
Jack Welch, Author
1935-Present

"Goals that are not in writing are not goals at all.
They are merely wishes or fantasies."
Brian Tracy, Author
1944-Present

"The best managers make decisions
on the basis of what is fair and equitable, not what is popular -
bearing in mind that not everyone will be pleased
with these decisions."
Priscilla Gross, Author

"Individuals don't win, teams do."
Sam Walton, Businessman
1918-1992

"It is better to offer no excuse than a bad one."
George Washington, U.S. President
1732-1799

"Don't be misled. Bad company corrupts good character."
Menander, Greek poet of Athens
342 B.C.-291 B.C.
Quoted by Paul in I Corinthians 15:33   KJB

Notes

Theme: Discernment

Motivations

"For the deliberations of mortals are timid, and uncertain our plans.
For the corruptible body burdens the soul
and the earthly tent weighs down
the mind with its many concerns.
Scarcely can we guess the things on earth, and
only with difficulty grasp what is at hand;
but things in heaven, who can search them out?
Or who can know your counsel,
unless you give wisdom and send your holy spirit from on high?
Thus were the paths of those on earth made straight, and people
learned what pleases you, and were saved by Wisdom."
Wisdom 9:14-18b   NABRE

"More tortuous than all else is the human heart,
beyond remedy; who can understand it?
I, the Lord, explore the mind and test the heart,
Giving to all according to their ways,
According to the fruit of their deeds."
Jeremiah 17:9-10 NABRE

"Search your hearts and be silent."
Psalms 4:4 NIV

"Make it your ambition to lead a quiet life,
to mind your own business
and to work with your hands."
1 Thessalonians 4:11-12 NIV

"Trust in the Lord with all your heart
and lean not on your own understanding."
Proverbs 3:5 NIV

"Do not be anxious about anything,
by prayer and petition, with Thanksgiving,
present your requests to God."
Philippians 4:6 NIV

Theme: Strength

My Shield

"Do not be afraid, for I am with you.
Don't be discouraged, for I am your God.
I will strengthen you and help you.
I will hold you up with my victorious right hand."

Isaiah 41:10   NLT

"Look toward the Lord.
Be radiant.
Let your face not be disappointed or ashamed."
Psalms 34:5

"Guard your heart. It is your duty.
It is the most difficult thing you will ever do."
Proverbs 4:23   NIV

"But thou, O Lord, art a shield for me...
I will not be afraid."
Psalms 3:3 and 6   KJV

"You are my defender and protector.
You are my God;
in you I trust."
Psalms 91:2   GNB

"You are my secret place and my breastplate against danger;
my hope is in your word."
Psalms 119:114   BEB

"I have set the Lord before me;
because He is at my right hand,
I shall not be moved."
Psalms 16:8   KJV

Theme: Children in Need

Practical Realities

Children are the stars of our lives,
They are our Star Dust!
But for children in need,
the universe in which they live, move, see, hear,
feel and think every day
is shaped by their practical realities:

abandonment, apathy, carelessness,
crime, feeling forgotten, harshness,
homelessness, hunger, illness,
emotional or learning disabilities,
loneliness, poverty, selfishness,
suicide, time, violence.

Do you see the children?
Where do you see them?
What are they doing?
home, work, school,
art, music, sports,
or on the street?

What's next?
Where are these children now?
What are their hopes and dreams?

Think about young mothers or fathers with children
who are scared and wondering
just how to make it.

Do they have a vision for the future?
How will they make it?
What are their practical realities?

Food, clothing, shelter,
faith, family, friends?
What choices will they have to make?

Children need individual attention,
person to person,
from real people,
in real time.
They "learn and grow
at different rates." [1]

Work to allow and to expand
their living and learning.
Pay attention
to their confidence
and self-esteem.
Avoid labels, limits and bias.

Reach out, "Go out and share.
Lead or serve.
Be an active participant in their
learning, growing and living." [2]
Show them visions of opportunities.
"Be a real Advocate." [1]
Be their Guiding Light!

When realities are recognized as actual, as very real,
as occurring every moment of every day,
rather than just as imaginings to create an idea,
then the need to over-analyze and over-engineer
could be significantly reduced.

A common sense and focused streamlining
of methods, processes and programs
would be a practical reality
for the advocates of children in need.

Work to advance and sustain the health, wellness,
education and safety of children.
Hold on to what is appropriate and proper.

In our responsibility, pray for wisdom.
Some things should not be negotiable.
Time is available, passes, and then is gone.
For one child,
how will time lost be recovered?
When for many children,
can time lost be recovered?

All they want is love and attention.
And, they want to survive!

Halt! Who goes there?

[1]Dr. Crystal Kuykendall, J.D., Speaker
American Association for Counseling and Development Convention
Reno, Nevada 1991

[2]Rev. Karl J. Daigle, Pastor

"Children need to be shown appreciation, approval and achievement
if they are to succeed in society."
Dr. Crystal Kuykendall, JD,
Educator, Counselor, Attorney, Speaker

"For we wrestle not against flesh and blood,
but against principalities, against powers,
against the rulers of the darkness of this world,
against spiritual wickedness in high places."
Ephesians 6:12   KJV

"For God did not appoint us to suffer wrath
but to receive salvation through our Lord Jesus Christ."
1 Thessalonians 5:9   NIV

"Life affords no greater responsibility; no greater privilege
than the raising of the next generation."
C. Everett Koop, Former U.S. Surgeon General
1916-2013

"If we lift the children, we lift the state...
The children come first."
Buddy Roemer, Former LA Governor
1943-Present

Theme: Contemplation

Quiet

Many individuals lead very busy lives.
How can we slow down and change?

Silence is difficult to enjoy
for more than a few moments.
Find those silent moments
throughout the day,
to still your mind, heart and body.
Rest quietly during travel time,
while waiting or standing in line.

Contemplation comes
through quieting and stilling ourselves.
Cultivate a habit of inner stillness.

Plan a Retreat.
Prepare.
Sit or lie down comfortably,
be alone, slow down, and calm down.

Be aware. Notice your surroundings;
recognize how you are feeling.
Very slowly, relax,
decrescendo from head to toe.

Breathe.
Take several long, deep breaths,
and time to disconnect
with the outside world.

Give thanks. Think only of the present moment,
simplify your wants and needs,
be content, be grateful.

Take care of yourself first.
Renew yourself,
so that you are there for others who need you.

At times, say No!
Carve out time
and save some for yourself.

Organize.
Eliminate clutter from your schedule.
Simplify your life.

Take Mini-Vacations.
Have fun. Enjoy every day.
Take more, or longer vacations.

Model a slower pace.
Do not neglect yourself.
Doing so would set a poor example for
 children, family, friends, students.

Slow down.
Simplifying your life is a process.
Bring change a single step at a time.

Start fresh,
through each moment of silence.

Ask yourself,
when and where will I be available
to listen to that inner message
meant just for me?

"An anxious heart weighs a man down,
but a kind word cheers him up."
Proverbs 12:25   NIV

"Self-control is strength.
Right thought is mastery.
Calmness is power."
James Allen. Philosopher/Writer
1864-1912
As A Man Thinketh, 1902

"In silence man can most readily preserve his integrity."
Fortune Cookie

"Silence is an integral element of communication;
in its absence, words rich in content cannot exist.
In silence, we are better able to listen to and understand ourselves;
ideas come to birth and acquire depth;
we understand with greater clarity what it is we want to say
and what we expect from others;
and we choose how to express ourselves."
Pope Benedict XVI
1927-Present
46th World Day of Communication
May 20, 2012

"My soul finds rest in God alone; my salvation comes from Him."
Psalms 62:1   NIV

Notes

Theme: Dreams

Reflection

I met Jesus once.
I was outside, near some trees.
He walked toward me and reached out.
I took his hand and he took mine.
No words were spoken. None were needed.

Once awake, I remembered the dream,
or was it really a dream?
A shiver, a chill, I'd felt.
I remember still.

The dream was real, was clear.
The memory is real, is clear.
No illusion, not imagined,
nothing virtual.

I did dream of such, although
no recall of having read of such.
Yet, with a small understanding only,
dreams neither forgotten nor ignored.

Consolement follows
resources from Above.
What experiences
have shaped your life?

"Be of good cheer! It is I; do not be afraid."
Matthew 14:27   NKJV

"And immediately, Jesus stretched out His hand and caught him
and said to him:
O, you of little faith, why did you doubt?"
Matthew 14:31   NKJV

"So we fix our eyes on not what is seen
but what is unseen.
For what is seen is temporary,
but what is unseen is eternal."
II Corinthians 4:18   NIV

"All I have seen teaches me to trust the creator
of all I have not seen."
Ralph Waldo Emerson, Writer
1803-1882

"What if you slept, and what if in your sleep you dreamed,
and what if in your dream you went to heaven
and there plucked a strange and beautiful flower,
and what if when you awoke you had the flower in your hand?
Ah, what then?"
Samuel Taylor Coleridge, Poet
1772-1834

Theme: Decision Making

Resolution

Be timely.
"When you are facing a change or
have a decision to make, instead of
saying you will do it tomorrow,
next week or next month or
when asking, when can I do it?
Why not do it now?" [1]

"Be firm, be strong [yet flexible]
like a redwood tree,
rather than bending and swaying with the wind,
like a reed of grass." [1]
[or like shifting sand.]

Have the courage everyday
to do what is right
with honesty, integrity and justice.
"You will have peace and freedom." [1]

[1] Rev. Richard Lombard
Associate Pastor

"The secret of change is to focus all of your energy
not on fighting the old,
but on building the new."
Socrates, Philosopher
469 BC – 399 BC
Athens, Ancient Greece

"Setting a goal is not the main thing.
It is deciding how you will go about achieving it,
and stay with that plan."
Tom Landry, Football Coach
1924-2000

"Never bend your head. Hold it high.
Look the world straight in the eye."
Helen Keller, Author
1880-1968

"People with clear written goals accomplish far more
in a shorter period of time
than people without them could ever imagine."
Brian Tracy, Author
1944-Present

"Successful leaders have a high sense of responsibility
over their lives."
George Barna with Bill Dallas
Master Leaders, p. 129
1955-Present

"Be the change you wish to see in this world."
Mahatma Gandhi, Father of India
1869-1948

Theme: Where Am I?

Revolution

Do you ask,
Where am I?
What am I doing?

You are here, now.
You have evolved to this point.
Are you in a rut?
"Are you so content with yourself
that you are in a state of self-delusion?
Get over yourself." [1]

What are your own needs?
"Do you not see the needs of others?
Are you missing outreach and service to others?" [1]

Are you ready for a difference?
You can make a change; you can move ahead.
"We learn, we grow, we evolve." [1]

You can have a revolution from within.
"You have a daily invitation to let others know" [1]
that you care and to tell them what they need to know,
with gentleness and reverence.

Sometimes, they may need to talk to us or just need to listen.
They may need encouragement, or just a little joyful noise.
But, it is the 'Good News' we always need to share.

"You can be excited that
you have this opportunity every day!" [1]
Have a revolution from within!
Create a difference.

You are the navigator.
You are at the helm.
You are steering the ship.
Where are you going?
Are you awake?

[1] Deacon Bill Roche, Deacon
Director of Faith Formation

"Good news makes you feel better.
Your happiness will show in your eyes."
Proverbs 15:30   NCV

"Everyone has inside of him a piece of good news.
The good news is that you don't know how great you can be!
How much you can love!
What you can accomplish!
And what your potential is!
Anne Frank, Author
1929-1945

"A life spent making mistakes is not only more honorable
but more useful than a life spent doing nothing."
George Bernard Shaw, Playwright
1856-1950

"For I know the plans I have for you,
plans to prosper you, and not to harm you,
plans to give you hope and a future."
Jeremiah 29:11   NIV

"Liberty cannot be established without morality,
nor morality without faith."
Alexis de Tocqueville, Historian
1805-1859

Notes

Theme: Foundation

$$S (x6) + R$$

So, how are you doing?

Remember, S (x6) + R.

Be Steady – consistent, not easily excitable, not easily upset.

Be Steadfast – loyal, unswerving, not easily swayed.

Be a Good Steward – well managed, entrusted with responsibility.

Be Strong – has will power, independent, with determined will.

Be Supportive – encourages, assists, holds up, argues for.

Be Spirit Led – do not be afraid. His mercy endures forever.

Be a Rock! – coherent, logical, orderly, silent, sticks together, supports bridges, the foundation for castles.

You now have the formula for success!

"And so I say to you, you are Peter and upon this rock I will build
my church, and the gates of the netherworld
shall not prevail against it."
Matthew 16:18   NABRE

"Be to me a rock, to which I may continuously come,
you have given the command to save me,
for you are my rock and my fortress."
Psalms 71:3   ESV

"The stone the builders rejected has become the cornerstone."
Psalms 118:22 and Acts 4:11   NIV

"Together, we are his house,
built on the foundation of the apostles and the prophets.
And the cornerstone is Christ Jesus himself."
Ephesians 2:20   NLT

"We are living stones."
Rev. Michael Thang'wa, FMH, Parochial Vicar
1972-Present

"The foundation stones for a balanced success are
honesty, character,
integrity, faith, love, and loyalty."
Zig Ziglar, Author and Speaker
1916-2012

Theme: Creation

Shadow

Within the Milky Way Galaxy,
the home of our Earth's solar system,
100,000 light years wide,
with our nearest galactic neighbor, Andromeda,
we each live every day.

Within this tiny place where we are,
we each have our own individual shadow.
Totally interesting, is that as
a living creature, even as we move,
our physical body remains visible
although our shadow does not.

However, shadows come and go
in the world of perpetual change,
ever changing, moving, growing,
diminishing, yet to fully disappear;
then, may return and only
for a speck of time.

The Shadow is given life
throughout our Universe
by the position of our Sun and
by our revolving Planet Earth,
all within the great and amazing Cosmos
in which our life exists and
in which we have our being.

The Shadow does not need time
for existence,
for it has perpetual change,
thus all the time in the world,
everlasting.

So, for the Shadow
there is a paradox.
"Oh-h-h, Shadow.
Time is never
time at all." [1]

[1] John Adam Harrington
1980-Present
Salt Box

"Paradox - promotes critical thinking;
contradictory but may be true."
Wikipedia

"You will do well to expand your horizons."
Fortune Cookie

"Someone is watching you from afar."
Fortune Cookie

"When men yield up the privilege of thinking,
the last shadow of liberty quits the horizon."
Thomas Paine, Author
1737-1809

"I believe in one God, the Father Almighty,
maker of heaven and earth,
of things visible and invisible."
The Nicene Creed
as noted by James Kiefer
1st Traditional Translation, 1549
2nd Modern Translation by
Intl. Committee on Liturgical Texts

Notes

Theme: Faith

So, Simple

"Consider what you do every day.
What is the center of your life?
Where do you spend the majority of your time and energy?" [1]

Where are you now?
What is on your list of things to do,
places to go and people to see?

When alone, or when with others,
wherever you are, reconsider self-imposed limitations.

Where do you want to be?
What do you want to be doing?

[1] Most Rev. Michael G. Duca, JCL,
Bishop, Diocese of Shreveport

"Now, faith is the substance of things hoped for,
the things not seen."
Hebrews 11:1 KJV

"Imagination rules the world."
Napoleon Bonaparte, Military Commander
1769-1821

"If you think you can or if you think you can't, you're right!"
Henry Ford, Industrialist
1863-1947

"Imagination is more important than knowledge."
Albert Einstein, Physicist
1879-1955

"One can never consent to creep when
one feels an impulse to soar."
Helen Keller, Author
1880-1968

"I tell you the truth, if you have faith as small as a mustard seed,
you can say to this mountain, 'Move from here to there'
and it will move.
Nothing will be impossible for you."
Matthew 17:20 NIV

Theme: Managing Change/Conflict

Strategy

Ready yourself to manage change and/or conflict.
Ever important is Integrity - your integrity,
and the integrity of the program.
If a change is forthcoming, communicate
and be straight forward.
Be aware. Don't withdraw communication.
Don't roadblock your employees.

Avoid predetermined decisions, ideas, or judgments,
which could cause a significant difference or
which could create an unnecessary or
a disconcerting impact.

Consider what is effective and what has worked well.
Collect, investigate, identify pertinent, appropriate,
and sufficient data, documentation or information
specific to the change or the conflict.
LISTEN!

Accept what is correct, valid and reliable.
Differentiate between right and wrong.
Be fair and flexible.

Recognize the direction people tend to move
in response to change or conflict,
toward others, away from others,
or against others.

Realize the benefits change could bring.
Describe any barriers as opportunities, rather
than as conflict and not only seek,
but identify and work on solutions.

Be aware that condescension or sarcasm
may bring about the fight or flight reaction
in individuals.

Discuss ideas not personalities.
Discourage blaming and whining.
Demonstrate care and develop understanding.
Remain open-minded and positive.

Review your plan, or the plan.
Review it from all angles.
Remember the value of keeping things simple,
but pay close attention to the details.

Simplify when appropriate.
The program will be only as good as the plan.
Avoid over engineering.
Notice and prevent unnecessary repetition or replication.

Catch yourself first -
don't interrupt your staff.
Stop and think. Don't micromanage.
Don't overreach.
Offer and allow opportunities for success.
Trust individuals to apply what they have been taught
and trained to do.
Trust them to do what they do best.

Have the courage every day to do what is right.
Be honest and consistent.
Show a strong sense of direction.
Reduce uncertainty in making decisions.
Build stability.

In summary,
when people believe what you say is true,
what you do is right, and that you care about them,
they will then follow you based on trust,
rather than based on fear.[1]

They will learn and grow and move forward
through change and also with greater ease
through and beyond conflict.

Motivate others!

[1] George Barna with Bill Dallas
1955-Present
Master Leaders, pp. 104 and 131

"Analyze only when necessary."
Fortune Cookie

"If you can't go forward and you can't go backward,
then go sideways."
Deborah Harris, Registered Dietitian
1956-Present

"Never neglect details.
When everyone's mind is dulled or distracted
the leaders must be doubly vigilant."
Colin Powell, Former Secretary of State
1937-Present

"A pessimist sees the difficulty in every opportunity;
an optimist sees the opportunity in every difficulty."
Winston Churchill, British Prime Minister
1874-1965

"Never go out to meet trouble.
If you just sit still, nine cases out of ten, someone will intercept it
before it reaches you."
Calvin Coolidge, U.S. President
1872-1933

"Let us train our minds to desire what the situation demands."
Fortune Cookie

"Have a rock solid team!"
Paul Navarre, Businessman, Speaker, Author

Sustainability

Change is constant.
Change is perpetual, ever evolving.
Change is universal.

On the other hand,
what on Earth is sustainable?

Sustainability, defined,
is the capacity to endure,
the capability of being continued
with minor or minimum long term effects
on the environment.

However, sustainability currently has
varied and multiple definitions.

The term should not be used flippantly,
as the latest trend in vocabulary;
moreover, to claim or to offer
sustainability as a serious possibility
should not be discussed lightly.

Both conflicts and constraints exist,
thus controversy.
Sustainability is not,
nor will ever be, easy.
What changes in life will then be sustainable?
The dust of the earth and God's heaven above.

"So, do not be dejected about change.
Move forward.

Do what you can every day.
Remember, success is made by
what we put into something,
not by what we get out of it." [1]

[1] Rev. Richard Lombard,
Associate Pastor

"Achieving sustainability will enable the earth to continue supporting life as we know it."
Wikipedia

"By fighting for an ideal,
we often bring about changes that make society better."
Paul King, Editorial Director
Food Service Director
Vol. 26 No.11, p. 9
11/15/2013

"Wise leaders have systems and people in place with a timeline and they don't allow themselves to hire someone by skipping or going around the process."
George Barna with Bill Dallas
1955-Present
Master Leaders, p. 73

"It is amazing how much a leader can get done
if he doesn't care who gets the credit."
George Barna with Bill Dallas
1955-Present
Master Leaders, p. 66

"True leadership equals humility, clarity and courage."
Anonymous

Notes

Theme: Support

Sustenance

Sustainability presents a continuous and serious challenge.
It depends upon sustenance with the development and
maintenance of specific, yet varied dimensions.

To classify a project, program or thing as "sustainable"
requires serious study, with a defined,
decided and determined plan.

With clear vision, ever sharp focus,
and sufficient care, find and know the needs,
and, with real honesty,
reality-check your motives.

Know, that not all ideas are fresh ideas,
not all ideas are good ideas,
not all ideas are practical ideas.
What may seem right,
may not be workable.

Identify what has worked quite well.
To that which is effective, efficient and correct,
hold on tight! Maintain it with diligence.
Work to improve and uphold the program.
Do not digress.

Do you plan to implement that idea or that change, or
are you just spinning your wheels?
You may realize this or you may not.
Sometimes, it is time to just move along,
but don't quit. Just move on.

Contingencies may serve no good purpose.
Don't cause difficulty for others,
either unnecessarily, or on purpose.
Decisions affect individuals.
Decisions and changes affect <u>real</u> people.

Review goals with stakeholders.
Questions asked must be answered.
Will the change or plan be workable?
What is the success rate? Do we know?
How do we know? How can we be certain?

Would change be for the good?
What are the intentions?
Immediate effects? Long term effects?
If there is serious reason to pause and reconsider,
then do it!

Sustainable projects seem to me
like weights on a scale of needs and wants.
An imperative need requires us
to be committed and to find solutions.

To realize the change,
visible and tangible results are needed.
The change demands that the work be done.
Complete and correct work produce change.
Sufficient support or sustenance allows
sustainability of the change.

Continue the change if it has value,
if it is right and good,
and if once accomplished
is in the best interest of our fellow man.
Protect, preserve and nurture it.

Are you ready to stand alone?
However, beware of blind ambition.
The path may not be easy.
You know that the path may not be straight and narrow,
but the vision will be ever so clear, crystal.

Then, when and why classify the change as "sustainable"?
Someone will need to do it.
There must absolutely be a way, and
there must be someone to continue it,
to support and sustain life and work.

Caution!
Let things not fall apart!

"Vanity of vanities! All is vanity."
Ecclesiastes 1:2 KJB

"Life is a battle between faith and reason
in which each feeds upon the other,
drawing sustenance from it and destroying it."
Karl Paul Reinhold Niebuhr, Theologian
1892-1971

"All a person's ways seem pure to them,
but motives are weighed by the Lord."
Proverbs 21:2 NIV

"Leaders bring danger within the arc of the shadow because they
diligently seek the truth, they unfailingly tell the truth,
and they won't settle for anything less than the truth."
George Barna with Bill Dallas
1955-Present
Master Leaders, p. 117

"Turning and turning in the widening gyre
the falcon cannot hear the Falconer;
things fall apart; the center cannot hold;
mere anarchy is loosed upon the world."
W.B. Yeats, Poet, Writer
1865-1939
"The Second Coming"

"Every man's way is right in his own eyes.
But the Lord weighs the hearts."
Proverbs 21:2 NASB

Theme: Deliberation

To Do or Not To Do?

Have a 'To Do' List?
Have a possible opportunity?
Have a new opportunity?
How do we decide to do something, or not?

Be open minded.
Weigh the benefits.
Compare the options.
Consider the value.
Practice creative thinking.
Discover the most workable solutions.

Ask, Am I interested?
Should I be interested?
Do I care about it?
Trust your instincts.
Do you trust it?
Pursue what you feel and know.

If trust is insufficient, or does not exist,
then re-group, re-think.
If you do not have adequate reference points to know any better,
then wait.
Ask, where do I go from here?
Proceed carefully.

Be open to words of advice.
Get objective opinions.
Acknowledge respected guidance.
Seek help and consider what is in your best interest.

You don't have to follow the latest thing or trend.
It is okay to disconnect.
It is okay to say, No!
If it doesn't feel right, don't do it.
Be assertive. Be firm.

Decide!
Accept the challenge!
Believe in it. Be motivated.
Get involved. Decide to do it.
Participate. Engage.

Build momentum. Be passionate.
Just do it - work it!
Stick to it - do more!
Finish it.

If you know there is something you need to do,
energize, and do it!
Move on through it and get it done!
HANDLE IT!

"Whilst we deliberate how to begin a thing,
it grows too late to begin it."
Quintilian, Roman Rhetorician
35 AD-100 AD

"Take time to deliberate,
but when the time for action has arrived,
stop thinking and go in."
Napoleon Bonaparte, Military Commander
1769-1821

"The road to happiness lies in two simple principles:
find what it is that interests you and that you can do well
and when you find it, put your whole soul into it –
every bit of energy and ambition and natural ability you have."
John D. Rockefeller, Businessman
1839-1937

"Doing what you love, whether it is having children,
working in a profession, being a nun, being a journalist,
is all - encompassing,
it is like a great love affair occurring every day.
It is not fun, not games, not winning or losing,
not making money or having your 15 minutes on television.
It is what no one can take away from you.
It is pure joy."
Georgie Anne Geyer, Journalist
1935-Present

"When in doubt, make a fool of yourself. There is a microscopically thin line between being brilliantly creative and acting like the most gigantic idiot on the earth.
So what the hell, leap."
Cynthia Heimel, Playwriter
1947-Present

"Do right and risk the consequences."
Sen. Sam Houston, Texas Army and the Governor of Texas
1793-1863

Theme: Transparency

Treatise on Words

I have been watching and listening to you for a long time. Beyond what is on my mind, there is a lot I want to say. You may wonder to whom I refer. While I have seen and heard those in need of encouragement and consolement, there are also those wanting to give help, as well as those who are giving help at this moment.

You can combine words to say whatever you want. Words can be so arranged and organized. They can be developed into simple or complex groupings - combinations to achieve your intended or desired purpose. Many times, with written words, it is beneficial to be parsimonious, while at other times, specificity may be quite in order or elaboration needed. Whether written or spoken, the language you choose can affect, and even change attitudes, and leave impressions. Words can have a tremendous and even historic impact, moreover, can be everlasting in a person's memory.

The words which you read can draw upon beliefs and imaginings and create internal feelings, either gradually or immediately. They can reach deep inside of you and grab thoughts and feelings, then circle back into your mind and create a response or reaction by what you say and do. Expressions from inside you can and may erupt and be looking straight back at you, which you must admit to yourself and/or to others. Then there are expressions which you cannot admit or even speak of aloud. Those feelings express an honesty from deep within. Thus, words can reach deeply into your soul or can chill you to the bone. Honesty with self has phenomenal power. What words are you hearing? What words do you hear right now? Wait, what is going on inside of you? Talk to yourself. Fix yourself first, before you try to fix others. Self-evaluation is quite valuable.

Some words can offer guidance, encouragement and positive thinking, such as: lighten up, let it go, do your best, be thankful, show gratitude, be excited, take care of yourself, be dedicated, listen attentively, care more, show compassion, you can do it, believe in yourself, or, I have faith in you.

Other words can define your emotions and your condition, or state-of-being. They tell others whether you are: happy, concerned, excited, sad, pleased, content, confused, peaceful, joyous, hopeful, worried, upset or lonesome. You can tell yourself and others if you feel: helpful, agreeable, determined, disappointed, tired, complacent, or like celebrating or giving up. With words you have an opportunity to make a joyful noise every day!

Be aware of and watch for messages that non-verbal communication presents to others. Body language and facial expressions both speak powerfully. Residual behaviors can have a significant impact; they may be long remembered and the mental images may remain. On the other hand, listeners can tire quickly of words spoken like a run-away freight train. The excess verbiage may neither be appreciated nor needed. Save the debate for those interested, or for a real competition.

Realize that "your attitude is transparent."[1] Through the words and body language you choose, people can sense what you really think and feel. Your attitude makes a visible difference! Do you find yourself finding fault with others? Adjust your focus.

At times, what is communicated comes not only from the words spoken, but from those words which were not spoken. Silence is obvious and can be quite loud. No matter how brief or lengthy, whether written, spoken, or unspoken, words have the power to create images in the mind.

Consider, not only how the words feel, but also how they sound. Words are invaluable tools with amazing power!

[1]Dr. Crystal Kuykendall, J.D.
Speaker, 1991 AACD Convention
150

"Before I speak, I have something important to say."
Groucho Marx, Comedian
1890-1977

"God, that all powerful Creator of nature and architect of the world,
has impressed man with no character so proper
to distinguish him from other animals,
as by the faculty of speech."
Quintilian, Roman Rhetorician
35 AD-100 AD

"As a man thinketh in his heart, so shall he be."
James Allen, Writer
1864-1912
As A Man Thinketh, 1902

"To thine own self be true, and it must follow, as the night the day,
then canst not thou be false to any man."
William Shakespeare, Poet
1564-1616

"But the things that come out of a person's mouth come from his heart..."
Matthew 15:18   NIV

"I keep telling myself to calm down, to take less of an interest in things
and not get so excited,
but I still care a lot about liberty,
freedom of speech and expression,
and fairness in journalism."
Kate Adie, Journalist
1945-Present

Notes

Theme: Truth

Truth

What are your priorities?
Have you taken time to evaluate?
What is truth?
Where is truth?

Ask: What are my strengths?
What are my weaknesses?
What have I done?
What have I failed to do?

If you have the ability to inspire and support others,
then use your ability.

"If Truth Were A Color"

"It would be gray and say nothing.
It would be red, like blood, showing pain.
It would be green, like money, with many riches.
If truth were a color...
It would be blue, filled with sadness.
It would be yellow, and cheerful.
It would be orange, having friendship.
If truth were a color...
It would be purple, like royalty.
It would be brown, and covered with mud.
It would be white, with fear and wonder.
If truth were a color...
It would be black, like the darkest place possible."

Camille Maree Chopin
1997-Present

"Then Peter proceeded to speak and said,
'In truth, I see that God shows no partiality.'"
Acts 10:34   NABRE

"In light of our own imperfections,
may we be generous with others."
Rev. Karl Bergin,
Pastor

"He who walks blamelessly does what is right
and speaks the truth in his heart."
Psalms 15:2-3   ESV

"I am the way and the truth and the life.
No one comes to the Father except through me."
John 14:6   NIV

"Pilate asked him, 'So you are a King?'
Jesus answered, 'You say that I am a King.
For this I was born, and for this I came into this world,
to testify to the truth.
Everyone who belongs to the truth listens to my voice.'
Pilate asked Him, 'What is the truth?'"
John 18:37-38   NRSV

Theme: Distractions

Waves

What holds exceptional meaning for you?
Do you love the beauty of nature?
Do you enjoy gazing at the night sky?
Are you inspired by the blowing of the wind?

Are people, places, pets,
music, art, literature,
sports, exercise,
hobbies or travel
a part of what you do?

In the course of your day
do you interact in real time,
talking, reading, writing,
painting, laughing, singing,
working, planting, resting?

Do small things make you happy,
noticing the simple things in life,
smiling, being happy,
laughing at yourself,
laughing with others?

Participate in the world every day.
Engage in life. Experience life without distractions.

Look over and beyond the waves:
no illusions, no obstacles,
nothing imaginary, nothing virtual.

Take time to live and breathe:
be true, genuine, authentic, spontaneous,
caring, sharing, nurturing.
Be as devoted in play,
as in work.

Take time for silence and contemplation.
What have you encountered
along your journey?

"Jesus said to Peter: Do not watch the waves.
Look at Me."
Matthew 14:22-36   KJV

"Obstacles are the things we see when we take our eyes off of
our goals."
Zig Ziglar, Motivational Speaker
1926-2012

"One always has enough time, if one will apply it well."
Johann Wolfgang von Goethe, Poet and Statesman
1749-1832

"We make a living by what we get. But we make a life by
what we give."
Winston Churchill, British Prime Minister
1874-1965

"Work is good provided you do not forget to live."
Bantu Proverb

"There is no greatness, where there is not simplicity, goodness,
and truth."
Leo Tolstoy, Acclaimed Novelist
1828-1910

Notes

Theme: Prayer

When

Whether alone or not,
quiet or not,
whether at mealtime, bedtime,
or at the break of day,

whether with wonder or celebration,
sadness or searching,
you talk to God.

When you engage
with Him in conversation,
you enter into
a personal relationship.

When you talk
to God,
it is very personal
and very real.

"Our Father which art in Heaven
hallowed be thy name.
Thy Kingdom come,
thy will be done in Earth,
as it is in heaven.
Give us this day our daily bread.
And forgive us our debts,
as we forgive our debtors.
And lead us not into temptation,
but deliver us from evil:
For thine is the kingdom
and the power, and the glory forever.
Amen."
Matthew 6:9-13   KJV

"In prayer, you enter into a personal relationship with God."
Rev. Joseph T. Fowler
Adminstrator

"Be joyful in hope, patient in affliction, faithful in prayer."
Romans 12:12   NIV

"God bless America,
God bless me,
God bless all of my family!
Amen."
Barbara Packard Lorio, RN, NICU
1938-Present

Theme: Listening

Whispers

"In this busy world
what do you hear?"[1]
Slow down and listen.

Do you hear your child,
spouse, parent,
sister, brother, neighbor, or friend?

"Are you listening?"[1]
Calm your mind.
Read. Listen to music. Take a walk.
Find a balance in this world of hurry.

What sounds do you hear - a rooster,
an owl, a mourning dove,
crickets, rain or wind?

A moment in life is needed to do nothing
and it is okay.

Get quiet.
Be patient. Wait.
"Retreat, Listen.
Who do you hear?
Who is speaking to you?" [1]

Listen to the Spirit.

[1]Deacon Bill Roche
Director of Faith Formation

"Let us be silent that we may hear the whisper of God."
Ralph Waldo Emerson, Writer
1803-1882

"The best remedy for those who are afraid, lonely or unhappy
is to go outside,
somewhere where they can be quiet, alone with the heavens,
nature,
and God.
Because only then does one feel that all is as it should be."
Anne Frank, Author
1929-1949

"My soul finds rest in God alone; my salvation comes from Him."
Psalms 62:1   NIV

"What was from the beginning,
what we have heard, what we have seen with our eyes,
what we looked upon,
and touched with our hands concerns the Word of Life."
1 John 1:1   NRSV

"So faith comes from hearing, and hearing through
the Word of Christ."
Romans 10:17   ESV
Hebrews 11:1   KJV

Theme: Service

Who Me?

Have you ever asked:
Who, me? Why me?
What can I do?
Can I do it?
Do I need to?
Do I want to?
Will I be alone?

"Know that you will not be alone." [1]
Don't wait for total understanding.
Open your heart and your mind.
Get out of the rut.
Move out of your comfort zone.
Accept challenges and grow.
"Achieve a dimension beyond yourself." [1]

"Do what you can
and God will do what He can.
The fruit of service is peace.
Others need help and support." [1]
If you are available,
reach out to others
according to their need.

Are you available?
Take the next step.

[1]Rev. Richard Lombard,
Associate Pastor

"The One who calls you is faithful and He will do it."
1 Thessalonians 5:24   NIV

"True Servant Leadership is all about
getting a handle
on our own selfishness."
George Barna with Bill Dallas
1955-Present
Master Leaders, p. 169

"I tell you the truth,
anything you did for even the least of my people here,
also you did for me."
Matthew 25:40   NIV

"And the peace of God, which transcends all understanding
will guard your hearts and your minds
in Christ Jesus."
Philippians 4:7   NIV

"And whatever you do, in word and deed,
do everything in the name of the Lord Jesus,
giving thanks to God the Father through Him."
Colossians 3:17   ESV

"God is not unjust; he will not forget your work
and the love you have shown him
as you have helped his people and continue to help them."
Hebrews 6:10   NIV

Theme: Metamorphosis

You

I have been thinking more about you.
You weigh heavily on my mind.

These are thoughts and ideas written for you,
in this time and space,
for your knowledge, experience and intuition,
toward our continuous struggle for good
and completeness.

Once we know our strengths and weaknesses,
it is our responsibility to improve,
it is our responsibility to do.
You know that I want the best for you
and that I have faith in you.
I know that you can do it.

It is my effort to introduce ideas for thought
toward contemplation and inspiration
for the change you want,
a change in behavior, evidence of learning,
the change to achieve all that you can,
and all that you can be,

A mind changing,
a life changing,
an "Oh, my God!" moment.

"No distance of place or lapse of time
can lessen the friendship of those who are thoroughly persuaded
of each other's worth."
Robert Southey, Poet
1774-1843

"Rules for Happiness:
Everyone needs something to do, someone to love
and something to hope for."
Immanuel Kant, Philosopher
1724-1804

"The only person over whom you have direct
and immediate control
is yourself.
The most important assets to develop, preserve and enhance,
therefore all your own capabilities.
And no one can do it for you. You must cultivate the habit
of leadership effectiveness for yourself –
and doing so will be the single best investment you will ever make."
Stephen R. Covey, Author
1932-2012

"A man sooner or later discovers that he is the master gardener of
his soul, the director of his life."
James Allen, Writer
1864-1912

Theme: Galvanize

Zn

30

Zn – Zinc, as defined: a chemical element, atomic number 30, atomic weight 65.37, symbol Zn.

Pure metallic zinc was discovered in 1746
by the German Chemist, Andrea Sigismund Marggraf.
It is used to protect the surface of metals,
and it galvanizes iron and steel.

Identified world zinc resources total about 1.9 billion tons.
Zinc is the 4th most common metal in use.
At the current rate of consumption, these reserves are
estimated to be depleted sometime between 2027 and 2055.

Zinc is essential for life.
It is an essential trace element in DNA and red blood cells.
For all living species, it maintains normal growth and development,
metabolism, the immune system, and heals wounds.

As Zinc galvanizes iron and steel,
and nourishes and protects human and animal growth,
it is my hope, with the words within this manuscript,
that the faith within you is nourished and galvanized
and will continue to build you to be ever stronger,
and protect you day after day,
to complete your success.

"Having a sense of purpose in your life
is the most important element of becoming
a fully functioning person."
Wayne Dyer, Psychologist and Author
1940-Present

"I don't believe any of us are too successful or too accomplished
to not be able to learn something new."
Robert Redford, Actor
1936-Present

"But as you excel in everything – in faith, in speech, in knowledge,
in all earnestness, and in our love for you –
see that you excel in this act of grace also."
II Corinthians 8:7   ESV

"Do not be conformed to this world,
but be transformed by the renewal of your mind,
that by testing you may discern what is the will of God,
what is good and acceptable and perfect."
Romans 8:28   ESV

"We shall not cease from exploration.
And the end of all our exploring will be to arrive where we started
and know the place for the first time."
T.S. Eliot, Major Poet
"Four Quarters"
1988-1965

"To waste, to destroy our natural resources,
to skin and exhaust the land
instead of using it so as to increase its usefulness,
will result in undermining,
in the days of our children,
the very prosperity which we ought by right
to hand down to them amplified and developed."
Theodore Roosevelt, U.S. President
1858-1919

Notes

Melodies for the Soul

"Sing unto him...
with instrument...a new song;
play skillfully with a loud noise...
the earth is full of the goodness of the Lord."
Psalms 33:2, 3, 5   KJV

"May the meditations of my heart
be pleasing in your sight oh Lord."
Psalms 19:14   NIV

"Those who wish to sing
always find a song."
A Swedish Proverb

Theme: The Key to Happiness

Accentuate the Positive

I remember that when my brother and I were young my Dad sang, at times, the song "Ac-Cent-Tchu-Ate The Positive". It was one of his favorite songs. He always sang it in its' entirety and I still know the words. He sang when we needed the instruction and message which the lyrics provided. He would go into song just because he loved the wonderful rhythm and the lively verse. Accent and duration of the melody and articulation of the words boosted the dynamics of this most memorable song!

When asked how things are going, he says "Things are improving." When asked how he is doing, he exclaims "I'm improving!"

Why deliberate?
Be resilient.
Be positive.
Share good news.
And accentuate the positive!

Lyrics from words of a Sermon by Rev. M. J. Devine's (1876-1965)
which inspired the 1944 song by
Johnny Mercer, Artist & Lyricist,
and Harold Arlen, Music.
Library of Congress
2015 National Recording Registry
Preserved at the Packard Campus
for Audio/Visual Conservation.

"A cheerful heart is good medicine."
Proverbs 17:22 NIV

Notes

Theme: Sunshine

"You Are My Sunshine"

I clearly remember my mother and me walking along a sidewalk one day, in downtown Shreveport, Louisiana. Ahead of us, and walking our way, was a gentleman who wore a business suit and a fedora. Of course, my mother recognized him immediately - Governor Jimmie Davis! In passing, he stopped and he shook my hand!

I still love the happy words and snappy tune of his song "You Are My Sunshine". When I hear either the melody or words, I still think of walking downtown, window shopping, and frequenting stores in Shreveport with my mother and meeting Governor Jimmie Davis.

May rays of sunshine fill your day, enough for you to share with those who pass your way!

"You Are My Sunshine"
Music and Melody written and performed by Oliver Hood, 1933.
Later performed by Jimmie Davis and Charles Mitchell.
Designated as a Louisiana State Song in 1977.

"Of all the music that reaches farthest into heaven, it is the beating of a loving heart."
Henry Ward Beecher, Speaker
1813-1887

Notes

Theme: The Blue Bird of Happiness

"Zip a Dee Doo-dah"

This was one of my favorite songs that I sang to my children, not only because it was delightful and so much fun, but also for the positivity conveyed in the message. All of my children have heard me sing it, especially when they needed to move a little faster. There were moments when they needed to hurry up, step it up, or just get it done!

So, I sang "Zip a Dee Doo-dah" to help us move forward with all of our plans and activities and to have a happy, very good, most wonderful day!

Song from the 1946 Disney movie "Song of the South,"
composed by Allie Wrubel,
with lyrics by Ray Gilbert.
Sung by James Baskett.

"And round thee with the breeze of song to stir
a little dust of praise."
Alfred Lord Tennyson
Poet Laureate of Britain
1809-1892

Notes

Nourishment for the Mind and Body

"Let food be thy medicine and medicine thy food."
Hippocrates, Physician
400BC-377 BC

"A mind always employed is always happy.
This is the true secret, the grand recipe for felicity.
The idle are only wretched.
In a world which furnishes so many employments which are useful,
and so many which are amusing,
it is our own fault if we ever know what ennui is."
Thomas Jefferson, U.S. President
1743-1826

"Unless you try to do something beyond
what you have already mastered,
you will never grow."
Ralph Waldo Emerson, Author
1803-1882

"Training your body helps you in some ways,
but serving God helps you in every way
by bringing you blessings in this life and in the future life, too."
1 Timothy 4:8   NCV

"The eyes of all wait for You,
You give them food in due season."
Psalms 145:16-17   WEB

Theme: Biscuits

"Going to Grandma's"

"I went to Grandma's house. It smelled old,
but it was pretty.
I saw the cat playing.
I felt Grandma's and Grandpa's hugs.
I heard the door closing.
The white biscuits tasted good.
When I go out and about, I like to go
to Grandma's house."

Kathryn Ann Chopin
1994-Present

"Let your conversation be always full of grace, seasoned with salt
so that you may know how to answer everyone."
Colossians 4:6   NIV

"One does not live by bread alone,
but by every word that comes from the mouth of God."
Matthew 4:4   NRSV

"Above all else guard your heart, for it is the wellspring of life."
Proverbs 4:23   NIV

"Heavenly Father, thank you for our family and our friends,
thank you for the meal we share and thank you for
the breath of air.
This we pray in Jesus name.
Amen."
Hyland Packard, Educator, Minister
1929-Present
Thanksgiving Prayer 2014

My Favorite
Glazed Lemon Cookies
(4 dozen)

1 ½ cups all-purpose flour
1/3 cup yellow cornmeal
½ tsp. baking powder
¼ tsp salt
½ cup unsalted butter, softened
½ cup granulated sugar
1 Tbsp. grated lemon rind
1 large egg
½ cup dried cranberries (optional)
½ cup pecans, chopped

Glaze:
1 cup confections' sugar
4-5 tsp. fresh lemon juice

Preheat oven to 350°
In a bowl, combine flour, cornmeal, baking powder and salt.
In a separate bowl, beat butter, sugar and lemon rind with an
electric mixer until fluffy. Beat in egg until blended. Beat in flour
mixture; stir in cranberries and nuts. Drop dough by teaspoonful
onto ungreased cookie sheets about 2 inches apart. Press tops with
a floured fork. Bake 10-12 minutes or until golden brown at edges.
Remove to wire racks to cool.

For the glaze, whisk confectioners' sugar and enough lemon juice to
make a thin glaze. Drizzle over tops of cookies. Let stand until glaze
sets.

"You have given us, O Lord, bread from heaven,
endowed with all delights and sweetness in every taste."
Wisdom 16:20   JB

"I am the living bread that came down from heaven."
John 6:51   NRSV

"I am the bread of life, says the Lord;
whoever comes to me will not hunger
and whoever believes in me will not thirst."
John 6:35   JB

"The water I give him will become in him a spring of water
welling up to eternal life."
John 4:14   NIV

"Like newborn infants, long for the pure, spiritual milk –
so that by it you may grow into salvation –
now that you have tasted that the Lord is good."
1 Peter 2:2   NRSV

Theme: Chocolate and Peanut Butter

Mimi's Peanut Butter Pie

8oz. light cream cheese, softened
½ cup peanut butter
1 ¼ cups confectioners' sugar
8 oz. Cool Whip (1 small container)
½ tsp. vanilla extract
1 - 9" graham cracker crust, or chocolate crumb crust
1/3 cup chocolate fudge sauce
Sweetened whipped cream

Set aside chocolate sauce, whipped cream and crust.
Blend all other ingredients together until smooth.
Spread chocolate sauce across bottom of crust.
Fold filling into crust and refrigerate.
To serve, garnish each slice with sweetened whipped cream and
drizzle with chocolate sauce.

They'll want more than one piece of pie! And you'll want to make
another pie very soon!!

Considering Nutrition and Exercise?
Be selective! Choose variety, moderation, and balance!

"Give about two hours every day, to exercise;
for health must not be sacrificed to learning.
A strong body makes the mind strong."
Thomas Jefferson, U.S. President
1743-1826

"I think we ought to concern ourselves with
making sure that our children are fit,
that they are concerned with being energetic –
that they use their young years not merely as spectators
but as participants in life."
John F. Kennedy, U.S. President
1917-1963

"Your boasting is not a good thing.
Do you not know that a little yeast
leavens the whole batch of dough?
Clean out the old yeast so that you may be a new batch,
as you are unleavened.
For our Passover lamb, Christ has been sacrificed,
therefore let us celebrate the Festival,
not with the old yeast of malice and evil
but with the unleavened bread of sincerity and truth."
1 Corinthians 5:6-8 NRSV, NIV

My Favorite
Lemon Meringue Pie

1 cup white sugar
3 Tbsp. all-purpose flour
3 Tbsp. cornstarch
¼ tsp. salt
1 1/3 cups water
½ cup lemon juice
2 tsp grated lemon rind

2 tbsp. butter
5 egg yolks, beaten
1 - 9" pie crust, baked
5 egg whites
6 tbsp. white sugar
½ tsp vanilla extract

Preheat oven to 350°F

Lemon Filling:
In a medium saucepan, whisk together 1 cup sugar, flour, cornstarch and salt. Stir in water, lemon juice and lemon rind. Cook over medium-high heat, stirring frequently, until mixture comes to a boil. Stir in butter. Place egg yolks in a small bowl and gradually whisk in ½ cup of hot sugar mixture. Whisk egg yolk mixture back into remaining sugar mixture. Bring to a boil and continue to cook while stirring constantly until thick. Remove from heat. Pour filling into baked pastry shell.

Meringue:
In a large, chilled, glass or metal bowl, whip egg whites until foamy. Add vanilla and add sugar gradually and continue to whip until stiff peaks form. Spread meringue over pie, sealing edges at crust. Bake 10 minutes in preheated oven or until golden brown.

My Aunt Sis always makes the best desserts, whether Lemon Meringue Pie, Fresh Pear Pie or Chocolate Crinkle Cookies!

"To succeed in life you need 3 things:
a wishbone, a backbone and a funny bone!"
Reba McEntire, Country Singer
1955-Present

"You catch more flies with honey than with vinegar."
Benjamin Franklin, Founding Father
1706-1790

"Use your talents. That's what they're intended for."
Fortune Cookie

"God...will not forget the work you did and the love you showed"
Hebrews 6:10   NCV

"I am the vine, you are the branches,
those who abide in me and I in them, bear much fruit."
John 15:5   NRSV

End Notes

Notes

_____

_____

_____

_____

_____

_____

_____

Theme: Deliberate Thought

Closing

It is important to finish.
Yet, we are never finished.
We continue to move forward
and we do not give up.
We are not yet perfect.

I always hope that you are okay
and are on the right path.
I have prayed for you every day,
Sometimes, all day,
at times, all night.

And now I seriously and sincerely
hope that these words,
created for you and
the power therein,
will transcend the metaphysical,
as well as all doubt and disbelief.

Truly, I care about you.
This time and effort
are an investment in your future.
You watch, you listen, you will see!
I believe for you!

"I returned, and saw under the sun,
that the race is not to the swift, nor the battle to the strong,
neither yet bread to the wise, nor yet riches
to men of understanding,
nor yet favor to men of skill, but time and chance
happeneth to them all."
Solomon, Author
Ecclesiastes 9:111 KJV

"I guide you in the way of wisdom and lead you
along straight paths."
Proverbs 4:11   NIV

"I am convinced that neither death nor life...
nor anything else in all creation,
will be able to separate us from the love of God that is in
Christ Jesus."
Romans 8:38-39   NIV

"This prefigured baptism, which saves you now.
It is not a removal of dirt from the body but an appeal to God
for a clear conscience, through the resurrection of Jesus Christ
who has gone into heaven and is at the right hand of God,
with angels, authorities, and powers subject to him."
1 Peter 3:21-22 NABRE

"He commands His angels to guard you."
Psalms 91:11   ESV

Theme: Beyond the Horizon

Who's Dust?

Am I okay?
At times, I have wondered if this is God's dust or my dust.

If not God's dust, then be it must, my own.
What surrounds you?
At times, do you wonder if you are okay?

We are responsible daily to learn, to develop
and to strengthen our individual abilities, skills and talents;
then to expand our minds and exercise our bodies
by continuing to think, read, write, teach, serve and work.

Fear not hard work
and fail not to enjoy your accomplishments.
We must search for and devote our time, energy and effort
toward worthwhile endeavors.

Draw up from deep inside,
your compassion
then deliver with action.
Thus, while here on earth
we will realize broader horizons,
sharper perspectives and have deeper insights.

Smile.
Be proud!
Be thankful for the dust you stirred
and Heaven sent!

"Liberty will not descend to a people;
a people must raise themselves to liberty;
it is a blessing that must be earned
before it can be enjoyed."
Charles Caleb Colton, Writer
1780-1832

"Never confuse movement with action."
Earnest Hemingway, Great Author
1899-1961

"We can do anything we want if we stick to it long enough."
Helen Keller, Author
1880-1968

"I have fought the good fight,
I have finished the race,
I have kept the faith."
II Timothy 4:7   ESV

"The God who gave us life gave us liberty."
Thomas Jefferson, U.S President
1743-1826

"And when you have reached the mountain top,
then you shall begin to climb."
Kahlil Gibran, Philosopher, Poet
1883-1931

Theme: Lastly

Forevermore

Imagine
life
forevermore
void
of
God's
goodness.

What
a
great
responsibility
we
have!

May
the
Lord
be
with
you.

"Only one life, 't will soon be past;
only what's done for Christ will last."
Charles Thomas "C.T." Studd
British Cricketer, Missionary
1860-1931

"For it was the morally informed commitment
and dedication of individual citizens
to worthy ideals of thousands of the free world
that led them on dangerous, lonely, often fatal missions
into the heart of Nazi darkness.
Without their dedication to moral and spiritual values,
that darkness might well have engulfed the world."
Robert Conroy Goldston, American History Writer
1927-1982

"You cannot imagine how it is when a whole country
breaks down completely."
Ellen Cremer Myers
Born 1925 Berlin, Germany
Jewish Official Translator

"I think 'thoughts of peace and not of affliction;'
you will call upon me and I will answer you;
and I will send back your captives from every place."
Summary: Jeremiah 29:11-14
Ref: RHE

"From everyone to whom much has been given,
much will be required."
Luke 12:48 NAS

"Multitudes who sleep
in the <u>dust</u> of the earth
will awake:
some to everlasting life."
Daniel 12:2   NIV

Notes

Inheritance

Inheritance
throughout time,
from men and women
came quotes
now and then,
old and new,
ever so many,
more than a few
with reason or rhyme
stood the test of time,
famous, legend, hero,
genius, beloved, revered,
eternal,
ours for all time.

The Chi Rho symbol with alpha and omega.

"Whatever you do, work heartily, as for the Lord and not for men,
knowing that from the Lord
you will receive the inheritance as your reward..."
Colossians 3:23-24 NIV

"...and they shall name him Emmanuel..." which means
"God is with us."
Matthew 1:23 NRSV

"For this reason Christ is the mediator...
receive the promised eternal inheritance...
now that he has died as a ransom to set them free from sins..."
Hebrews 9:15 NIV

"There is one body and one Spirit,
just as you were called to the one hope of your calling,
one Lord, one Faith, one baptism, one God and Father of all,
who is above all and through all and in all."
Ephesians 4:4-6 NRSV

"Be still and know that I am God."
Psalms 46:10 KJV

". . . teaching them to observe all that I have commanded you.
And behold, I am with you always, until the end of the age."
Matthew 28:20 NABRE

Bibliography:

"4 B Light-Years Long. Largest Structure in the Universe Discovered." 1/11/2013: Monthly Notices of the Royal Astronomical Society.

"Accentuate the Positive" – Wikipedia

A Treatise Concerning the Principles of Human Knowledge. "Introduction." George Berkeley, published 1710.

BLINK: The Power of Thinking Without Thinking, Malcolm Gladwell, pg. 276. 2005: Little, Brown and Company, Hachette Book Publishers, NY, NY. Used by permission.

"Caffeine." 2/8/2013: Federal Register, Vol. 78, No. 27, pg. 9539. Part III, Department of Agriculture, Food and Nutrition Service.

"Hettler Urges Counselors to Set Example for Society," William Hettler. 5/1991: Guidepost, pgs. 17 & 18. American Association for Counseling and Development, 5999 Stevenson Ave, Alexandria, VA.

"Learning Lessons," Buddy Roemer (Former Governor of Louisiana). March/April 1991: Louisiana Life, Baton Rouge, LA.

Life Is So Good, George Dawson and Richard Glaubman, pgs. 223-224. 2013: Random House, Inc. NY, NY.

Master Leaders, George Barna with Bill Dallas, 2009: George Barna, pgs. 66, 73, 91, 111, 117, 129, 104, 131, 161, and 169. The Church Communication Network, Published in Association with Fedd and Co., Inc., Brentwood, Tennessee. Used by permission.

"Obliterate Obstacles to Wellness, Tear Down Bias," Crystal Kuykendall. 5/1991: Guidepost, pgs. 16 and 18. American Association for Counseling and Development, 5999 Stevenson Ave., Alexandria, VA.

<u>Sinister Touches: The Secret War Against Hitler</u>, Robert Conroy Golston, pg. 199. 1982: The Dial Press, NY, NY.

"Sustainable Future," Paul King, Editorial Director. <u>Food Service Director</u>, pg. 9, Vol. 26, No. 11.

<u>The Cornerstone Report</u>.
http://conservationreport.com/2010/01/09/quote-we-live-on-a-mote-of-dust.

"The Dodo Bird," Hiliare Beloc. Published 1896: <u>The Bad Child's Book of Beasts</u>, pgs. 27-30.

"What's In a Definition?" JBL. 4/2013: <u>Food Management</u>, pg. 8. Penton Media, Inc. Overland Park, Kansas.

"Why Laughter is Good for You," Glenn Plaskin, Contributing Editor. 2/2013: <u>Family Circle Magazine</u>, pgs. 62-63. NY, NY

"You are My Sunshine" – Wikipedia

"Zip A Dee Doo-Dah" - Wikipedia

CPSIA information can be obtained
at www.ICGtesting.com
Printed in the USA
BVHW07s1559031018
529147BV00014B/1236/P